D0204771

EUROPE AND THE JAPANESE
CHALLENGE

Europe and the Japanese Challenge

*The Regulation of Multinationals in
Comparative Perspective*

MARK MASON

OXFORD UNIVERSITY PRESS
1997

Oxford University Press, Great Clarendon Street, Oxford OX2 6DP

Oxford New York
Athens Auckland Bangkok Bogota Bombay
Buenos Aires Calcutta Cape Town Dar es Salaam
Delhi Florence Hong Kong Istanbul
Karachi Kuala Lumpur Madras Madrid Melbourne
Mexico City Nairobi Paris Singapore
Taipei Tokyo Toronto Warsaw
and associated companies in
Berlin Ibadan

Oxford is a trade mark of Oxford University Press

Published in the United States by
Oxford University Press Inc., New York

British Library Cataloguing in Publication Data
Data available

Library of Congress Cataloging in Publication Data
ISBN 0-19-829264-3
Data available

1 3 5 7 9 10 8 6 4 2

Typeset by Best-set Typesetter Ltd., Hong Kong
Printed and bound in Great Britain by
Biddles Ltd, Guildford and King's Lynn

To Roslyn

Acknowledgements

RARELY has an author of a book enjoyed the benefit of so much insightful counsel from so many leading thinkers located throughout the world as has this author in preparing this book. Colleagues from Europe, Japan, and the United States contributed to the design of the initial project, the crafting of the methodology, and the interpretation of the research results.

Although it would be practically impossible to list all the scholars and others who so generously contributed their ideas and insights, I would like to single out for special thanks a number of academic colleagues whose thinking has had a particularly important impact on this work: Edward Graham (Institute for International Economics), Stephen Guisinger (University of Texas at Dallas), Geoffrey Jones (University of Reading), Akira Kudo (University of Tokyo), Simon Nuttall (College of Europe), Hugh Patrick (Columbia University), Simon Reich (University of Pittsburgh), Jonathan Story (INSEAD), Raymond Vernon (Harvard University), Ezra Vogel (Harvard University), and Mira Wilkins (Florida International University). In addition, it is a special pleasure to acknowledge the many contributions of Dennis Encarnation, now at Harvard University's Kennedy School of Government, whose generosity and genuine interest in ideas have so greatly enhanced the depth and breadth of this work.

At Oxford University Press, I am grateful to David Musson, Editor of Management and Business Studies, who expertly guided the manuscript through the many involved stages from submission of the original text to review, revision, editing, and ultimate publication. Also at Oxford, I am pleased to acknowledge the outstanding contributions of Leonie Hayler, Assistant Editor of Business and Linguistics, who coordinated the overall preparation of the text for publication, and Jacqueline Pritchard, who copy-edited the manuscript. Finally, I wish to thank the external (and, to me, anonymous) reviewers consulted by Oxford University Press in connection with this work. These reviewers offered very thoughtful and constructive feedback on the manuscript.

It also gives me pleasure to acknowledge the support of several institutions whose financial and other assistance proved crucial at various stages of research, analysis, and write-up. Chief among these are the School of Management at Yale University, the European Institute of Business Administration (INSEAD) and its Euro-Asia Centre, the Alfred P. Sloan Foundation, and the Alex C. Walker Educational and Charitable Foundation.

Finally, I would like to thank my family. My parents, as always, provided both inspiration and support. And my wife Roslyn, to whom this book is dedicated, offered her characteristically enthusiastic encouragement from the start of the project to its ultimate completion.

M.M.

Contents

List of Tables

List of Figures

Abbreviations

ACEA	Association des Constructeurs Européens d'Automobiles (Association of European Automobile Manufacturers)
BOT	Board of Trade (United Kingdom)
CCMC	Comité des Constructeurs du Marché Commun (Committee of Common Market Manufacturers)
CD	compact disc
CFIUS	Committee on Foreign Investment in the United States
CTV	color television
DTI	Department of Trade and Industry (United Kingdom)
EC	European Community
1BCD	First Banking Coordination Directive
FCC	Federal Communications Commission (United States)
FDI	foreign direct investment
FEFTCL	Foreign Exchange and Foreign Trade Control Law (Japan)
FIL	Foreign Investment Law (Japan)
IMVP	International Motor Vehicle Program
JAMA	Japan Automobile Manufacturers Association
MITI	Ministry of International Trade and Industry (Japan)
MNC	multinational corporation
MOF	Ministry of Finance (Japan)
NYK	Nippon Yusen Kaisha
OECD	Organization for Economic Cooperation and Development
OEM	original equipment manufacturer
PAL	phased alteration lines
PRO	Public Records Office
2BCD	Second Banking Coordination Directive
SCAP	Supreme Commander for the Allied Powers
SEA	Single European Act

SECAM	séquence couleur à mémoire
VCR	videocassette recorder
VER	voluntary export restraint
VRA	voluntary restraint agreement
YSB	Yokohama Specie Bank

Introduction: Europe and the Japanese Challenge

JAPANESE foreign direct investment (FDI) surged into the United States and Europe beginning in the late 1980s. Encouraged by the rapid appreciation in the value of the yen, growing threats of overseas protectionism, and other factors, Japanese firms invested unprecedented amounts of capital in the economies of Japan's two Triad partners. In the United States, Japanese companies directly invested some $113 billion between 1987 and 1991 alone, an amount which exceeded accumulated flows of Japanese FDI to America between 1951 and 1986 by a factor of three.[1] These spectacular inflows had catapulted Japan to the position of largest foreign direct investor in the United States by 1992.[2]

Japanese direct investments soon rose dramatically in Europe as well.[3] Following gradual expansion during the 1970s, Japan's FDI beginning in the late 1980s and continuing into the early 1990s entered Europe at rates which far exceeded earlier levels. Cumulative flows of Japanese FDI to Europe amounted to less than $30 billion in 1986, for example, but had increased to more than $83 billion by 1993.[4] The United Kingdom received a disproportionate amount of this investment, yet in comparison with earlier years, Japanese FDI had accumulated appreciably in all the principal economies of Europe by the early 1990s.[5] And although Japan's FDI poured into America more quickly than into Europe, by the early 1990s Japanese firms had managed to acquire substantial stakes in a host of European sectors. Finance and insurance, manufacturing and trade attracted the largest quantities of Japanese FDI in the region.[6]

AMERICAN DEBATE, AMERICAN RESPONSE

The rapid increase of Japanese FDI in the United States sparked an intense debate over the implications of Japan's growing economic presence and appropriate American policy responses. Sensational popular books, for example, argued that levels of Japanese direct investment in the United States were reaching dangerous proportions—and that the US government had to react accordingly.[7] Rising Japanese stakes in the American economy, some warned, threatened the US tax base, its technological leadership, and the quality and overall quantity of US jobs.[8] Others feared that such FDI would enable Japanese business to wield undue influence over US policymaking and even jeopardize American national security.[9] Based on these and other fears, a number of observers argued that the US government should carefully screen potential Japanese (and other) FDI before permitting its entry into the United States.[10] Others went still further, suggesting that American authorities adopt a policy of reciprocity towards Japanese FDI, or that American officials should impose performance requirements on Japanese direct investors in the United States.[11]

By contrast, students of a very different school of thought emphasized the potential benefits Japanese FDI created for the US economy. These benefits, they argued, included the supply of fresh sources of investment capital, creation of new jobs, expanded tax revenues from the domestic operations of Japanese-owned firms, the transfer of cutting-edge management methods and other firm-specific assets, and the stimulation of healthy competition on American shores.[12] Greater investment in the US economy from any source improved overall US economic performance, students of this school argued, so US policy should not impede Japanese FDI but rather promote its unencumbered access to American markets.[13]

With few exceptions, by the early 1990s it had become clear that those who favored the maintenance of open US policies towards FDI from Japan (and elsewhere) had prevailed. At the national level, explained a leading economic policymaker in the Bush Administration, the United States generally 'adopted and maintained open investment policies because they serve our national interest. Open investment flows advance US economic efficiency,' he continued, 'promote economic growth, strengthen US industrial competitiveness, and foster higher living standards for all Americans.'[14] The only important exception to this overall US policy approach during the period was adoption of the so-called Exon–Florio Amendment to the 1988 Trade Act.[15] This amendment empowered the Committee on Foreign Investment in the United States (CFIUS), a federal inter-agency group with little prior authority, to review and, at presidential direction, restrict mergers, acquisitions, and takeovers which posed a direct threat to national security. Such restrictions were rarely invoked in subsequent years, however, and still more rarely involved proposed Japanese direct investments in the United States.[16]

Indeed, at the state level, government policies often were designed actively to *encourage* FDI from Japan and elsewhere. Competing against other US states to attract potential Japanese investments to their locales, state governments across the country tried to outbid each other by offering better tax breaks and other superior incentives to lure Japanese companies. The record of the automobile industry, as discussed below, stands as a case in point. It is true that state-specific regulations in the banking and certain other sectors may well have limited Japanese FDI in some instances, yet in general American states eagerly courted direct investments from Japan.[17]

EUROPEAN DEBATE, EUROPEAN RESPONSE

Large inflows of Japanese FDI also stimulated lively debate across Europe. Much of this debate echoed concerns raised in the 1960s over the rapid build-up of US FDI in Europe, as captured in the popular book *Le défi américain* (The American Challenge).[18] 'Fifteen years from now,' French journalist Jean-Jacques Servan-Schreiber had warned in the opening passages of that 1967 polemic, 'it is quite possible that the world's third great industrial power, just after the United States and Russia, will be not Europe, but *American industry in Europe*.'[19] The rapid post-war expansion of American multinationals in the region threatened the economic and political sovereignty of Europe, he and others had asserted, and Europe therefore was compelled to respond.

Some two decades later, many Europeans argued that they confronted a no less daunting 'Défi japonais' (Japanese Challenge) which required strong, coordinated policy responses to defend European interests against rising investments and related economic competition from Japan.[20] Popular books such as *L'Étreinte du samourai: Le Défi japonais* (The embrace of the samurai: the Japanese Challenge) and *Le Japon achète le monde* (Japan buys the world) excited the passions of many in France and elsewhere in Europe, as did front-page stories in major European magazines and newspapers with titles such as 'The Rising Sun over Europe' and 'Comment le Japon nous envahit' ('How Japan is invading us').[21] Popular fears were echoed by many leading political figures across the Community, though few were more outspoken than French Prime Minister Édith Cresson: 'The Japanese have a strategy of world conquest,' she proclaimed in the midst of the Japanese investment boom. 'They have finished their job in the US. Now they're about to devour Europe.'[22]

As in the United States, however, Japanese foreign direct investors also found numerous supporters in Europe. Many European economists, for example, underlined the potential advantages of increased Japanese FDI in their region in much the same way their American colleagues stressed the benefits of such investments for the United States.[23] Influential segments of the British media in particular likewise pointed to the potential contributions of Japanese investment in strengthening EC-based industry and otherwise improving the economic performance of the Community. And leading politicians such as British Prime Minister Margaret Thatcher spoke up forcefully in favor of the advantages of inward FDI from Japan.[24]

The simultaneity of the Japanese Challenge and ongoing European efforts to achieve greater regional integration raised additional policy questions for host governments and regional European agencies. Adoption of the Single European Act (SEA) in 1986 committed all twelve EC member states to adopt certain common policies and to cede various powers to Community institutions beginning January 1, 1993. This so-called Europe 1992 program challenged both the nature of the region's traditional policymaking processes and the eventual means through which resulting policies would be implemented. What roles, for example, would the European Commission and individual member states play in negotiating with official Japanese counterparts and crafting relevant European policies towards inward FDI from Japan?[25] And would the Community or individual member states assume responsibility for implementing such policies?

COMPARATIVE PERSPECTIVES

Although America's policy responses to the 'Japanese Challenge' have been examined extensively, less understood and less well analyzed are the relative character and larger meanings of Europe's ultimate policy formulations.[26] What specific policy initiatives would European authorities adopt in response to growing direct Japanese competition in home markets? How would these policies compare to analogous American responses, and what underlying factors might help explain any major differences between the American and European approaches? Would the nature of European policymaking towards the greater Japanese Challenge point to a more general pattern or model?

Answers to these questions could in turn provide fresh insights into far broader conceptual debates over the evolution of capitalism as it is practiced in different national or regional settings. In recent years, of course, a growing number of scholars and others has argued that globalization, increasing economic interdependence, and related factors have eroded differences between the capitalist systems of the advanced industrialized countries. From the organization of production to the regulation of domestic financial systems to responses towards international competition, it is argued, international forces are propelling the industrialized world's varied capitalist systems towards global convergence.[27]

The case of inward direct investment offers an unusual opportunity to test one important aspect of this larger convergence hypothesis. After decades of increasing flows of international capital, convergence theory would suggest that by the early 1990s Europe and America should have treated inward FDI in substantially similar ways. By systematically comparing and contrasting European and American responses towards surging direct investment inflows from Japan, this study will gauge the degree of similarity in the recent responses of these two major capitalist economies as each confronted a similar competitive threat from abroad.

Moreover, the application of this test can be extended to include the entire Triad of advanced industrialized economies. Indeed, just as Europe and the United States confronted their Japanese 'challenges' beginning in the late 1980s, throughout these years Japan continued its decades-long struggle over how best to respond to the threat of large potential inflows of FDI from Europe and America. By incorporating the Japanese experience into this larger record, it will then be possible to assess the degree to which convergence has actually occurred in the responses adopted by each of the three capitalist economies of the Triad towards this critical dimension of international economic competition.

METHODOLOGY

To explore these and related issues, this book will systematically analyze critical instances of European policymaking towards inward direct investment from Japan in comparative perspective. Following a historical overview of the development of Japanese FDI in Europe and a comparison with its development in the United States, this work will examine in comparative terms the nature of the European policy response in three major sectors as Japan's investments mounted and completion of Europe's 1992 program approached.

These three sectors—automobiles, consumer electronics, and banking—were chosen for a number of important reasons. First, Japanese multinationals directly invested very large sums of capital in these industries in Europe beginning in the late 1980s. Second, these sectors each represented hugely important facets of the European economy, and therefore demanded serious scrutiny by Europe's policymakers. Third, by including banking as well as automobiles and consumer electronics, this study will explore European policy responses not only in the manufacturing sector but in the vitally important services sector as well. And fourth, the development of significant inflows of Japanese FDI in the same host sectors in the United States facilitates more precise, industry level comparisons between European and American policy reactions.

To sharpen comparisons across different sectors within Europe, each industry chapter is organized in a similar fashion. First, the specific European industrial context prior to the advent of the capital surge from Japan is analyzed, together with the development of

Japanese strategies in the region and evolving European policy responses. Second, the process and outcomes of European policy-making towards inflows of Japanese FDI in each sector during the great investment surge are examined. And third, each industry chapter then compares European policies with their respective American analogs.

The concluding chapter draws together empirical evidence from preceding chapters, identifies broader policy patterns, and then explores the still wider implications of this evidence for ongoing debates over the evolution of alternative forms of capitalism in the advanced industrialized countries. The general nature of the official European response to inward FDI from Japan in automobiles, consumer electronics, and banks is analyzed and compared to the analogous American policy formula. This chapter then defines a more general European policy model towards the Japanese Challenge based on a set of specific contextual features. Finally, the character of the European response is placed in still broader international perspective by considering as well Japanese responses designed to confront potentially large direct investment inflows from abroad. The different responses of the European, American, and Japanese political economies towards inward FDI are then related to wider conceptual debates over the convergence of capitalist systems across the Triad.

NOTES

1. Ministry of Finance (Japan). Data calculated on approvals basis and fiscal years, which begin April 1.
2. US Department of Commerce, *Survey of Current Business*. Position data calculated on historical cost basis.
3. Unless otherwise indicated, throughout this book 'Europe' refers to the European Community (now the European Union).
4. Ministry of Finance (Japan).
5. According to official Japanese statistics, as of March 31, 1993—a date roughly co-terminous with the endpoint of this study of Europe prior to completion of the Single Market—the United Kingdom had received the largest share of Japanese FDI stocks (38%), followed by the Netherlands (21%), Germany (9%), Luxembourg (8%), France (7%), Switzerland (4%),

Spain (3%), Belgium (3%), Italy (2%), and other Europe (5%). Ministry of Finance (Japan).

6. The sectoral breakdown of accumulated flows of Japanese FDI to Europe, as of March 31, 1993, was: Finance and Insurance (38%), Manufacturing (23%), Trade (13%), Real Estate (12%), Miscellaneous Services (7%), and Other (7%). Ministry of Finance (Japan).

7. See, for example, Daniel Burstein, *Yen! Japan's New Financial Empire and its Threat to America* (New York: Simon & Schuster, 1988) and Douglas Frantz and Catherine Collins, *Selling Out: How We are Letting Japan Buy our Land, our Industries, our Financial Institutions, and our Future* (Chicago: Contemporary Books, 1989).

8. See, for example, Martin and Susan Tolchin, *Buying into America: How Foreign Money is Changing the Face of our Nation* (New York: Times Books, 1988). Arguments about the tax base generally were linked to the contention that some Japanese firms engaged in transfer pricing to avoid paying proper amounts of taxes in the United States. *Institutional Investor* (Oct. 1990), 7 and *Business International Money Report*, July 23, 1990.

9. For instance, see Pat Choate, *Agents of Influence: How Japan's Lobbyists in the United States Manipulate America's Political and Economic System* (New York: Knopf, 1990).

10. See, for example, Norman Glickman and Douglas Woodward, *The New Competitors: How Foreign Investors are Changing the US Economy* (New York: Basic Books, 1989) and Felix Rohayton, 'America's Economic Dependence,' *Foreign Affairs*, 68: 1 (1989), 53–65.

11. On reciprocity proposals, see, in particular, Clyde V. Prestowitz, Jr., *Trading Places: How We Allowed the Japanese to Take the Lead* (New York: Basic Books, 1988). On arguments for performance requirements, see Glickman and Woodward, *The New Competitors*; Robin Gastner, 'Protectionism with Purpose: Guiding Foreign Investment,' *Foreign Policy*, 88 (Fall 1992), 91–106; and Prestowitz, *Trading Places*. More nuanced were the policy prescriptions of Laura D'Andrea Tyson—a senior official in the first Clinton Administration—who argued for a policy of 'cautious activism' which combined monitoring of FDI with selective use of reciprocity in 'They Are Not Us: Why American Ownership Still Matters,' *American Prospect* (Winter 1991), 37–49.

12. See, among many other contributions, Richard Caves, 'Japanese Investment in the United States: Lessons for the Economic Analysis of Foreign Investment,' *World Economy*, 16: 3 (May 1993), 279–300; John Makin, 'The Effects of Japanese Investment in the United States,' in Kozo Yamamura (ed.), *Japanese Investment in the United States: Should We Be Concerned?* (Seattle: Society for Japanese Studies, 1989), 41–62; and, more generally, Edward Graham and Paul Krugman, *Foreign Direct Investment in the United*

States (3rd edn., Washington, D.C.: Institute for International Economics, 1995).

13. Robert Reich popularized these arguments in his influential article 'Who is Us?,' which asserted that the location of production rather than the nationality of ownership defined America's critical interest regarding investments by multinationals based in Japan or anywhere else. In a world in which firms acted in their self interest rather than in the national interest, Reich argued, 'we must open our borders to investors from around the world rather than favoring companies that may simply fly the US flag.' Robert Reich, 'Who is Us?,' *Harvard Business Review* (Jan.–Feb. 1990), 54.

14. Roger B. Porter, 'United States Investment Policy,' *Vital Speeches of the Day*, 58: 3 (Dec. 15, 1991), 1–2.

15. In addition, the US historically has limited FDI in various federally regulated industries. See below.

16. Indeed, through mid-1994 the CFIUS formally blocked just one proposed FDI project, which involved an attempted acquisition of an American firm by a Chinese company. And in only five cases were proposed investments withdrawn before the CFIUS took formal votes. Of these five cases, just two involved Japanese investors. See Graham and Krugman, *Foreign Direct Investment in the United States*, 129–31.

17. Ibid., 140–4. In response to the Japanese investment surge, a number of American states did introduce bills in the late 1980s to monitor or control inward FDI. Virtually all of these proposed bills, however, failed to gain legislative approval. See, for example, Cheryl Tate, 'The Constitutionality of State Attempts to Regulate Foreign Investment,' *Yale Journal*, 99: 8 (June 1990), 2030–2.

18. Jean-Jacques Servan-Schreiber, *Le Défi américain* (Paris: Denoel, 1967); trans. as *The American Challenge* (New York: Atheneum, 1968).

19. Servan-Schreiber, *The American Challenge*, 3.

20. Throughout this book, the term 'Japanese Challenge' refers to the surge of Japanese FDI and related exports to Europe and the United States principally during the late 1980s and early 1990s.

21. 'The Rising Sun over Europe,' *International Management* (July–Aug. 1989), 14–20; 'Comment le Japon nous envahit,' *L'Express*, June 20–6, 1991.

22. As quoted in *Business Week* (June 3, 1991), 44.

23. See, for example, Stephen Thomsen and Phedon Nicolaides, *The Evolution of Japanese Direct Investment in Europe: Death of a Transistor Salesman* (London: Harvester Wheatsheaf, 1991) and, for a relatively early and somewhat more cautious endorsement of Japanese FDI in one principal European host, see John Dunning, *Japanese Participation in British Industry* (Beckenham: Croom Helm, 1986). Qualified support for Japanese FDI in Europe is also expressed in Stefano Micossi and Gianfranco Viesti, 'Japanese Direct Manufacturing Investment in Europe,' in L. Alan Winters and

Anthony J. Venables (eds.), *European Integration: Trade and Industry* (New York: Cambridge University Press, 1991) and Roger Strange, *Japanese Manufacturing Investment in Europe: Its Impact on the UK Economy* (London: Routledge, 1993). For a Japanese viewpoint, see Kenjiro Ishikawa, *Japan and the Challenge of Europe 1992* (London: Pinter for the Royal Institute of International Affairs, 1990).

24. See, for example, *Independent*, Sept. 28, 1990. More generally, see 'Japanese Investment in the 1990s: How British Leaders React,' *Anglo-Japanese Journal*, 4: 1 (Apr.–June 1990), 6–13.

25. By treaty, the European Commission had no formal authority to regulate FDI. As we shall see, however, in practice it managed to influence such investments through a variety of methods.

26. For a comprehensive treatment of US policy towards inward FDI from Japan and elsewhere, see Graham and Krugman, *Foreign Direct Investment in the United States*. On the development in the United States of Japanese FDI in particular and its implications for US–Japanese trade, see Dennis Encarnation, *Rivals beyond Trade: America versus Japan in Global Competition* (Ithaca, NY: Cornell University Press, 1992). An early attempt to generalize about the European policy record, specifically as it relates to inflows of Japanese manufacturing FDI, is Gastner, 'Protectionism with Purpose.' See also the several contributions in Mark Mason and Dennis Encarnation (eds.), *Does Ownership Matter? Japanese Multinationals in Europe* (Oxford: Oxford University Press, 1994).

27. For example, overwhelming global forces, many adherents of convergence thought would argue, are pushing the advanced industrialized countries to adopt increasingly similar policies towards external competition. According to the noted economist Lester Thurow, for example, 'In a global market all of the pressures are to harmonize down—much as we see American states competing to induce business firms to locate in their jurisdictions by giving them special tax breaks. The jurisdictions with low taxes or few regulations are under no pressure to change,' Thurow stated, but 'the jurisdictions with many regulations or high taxes are under a lot of pressure to change.' Lester Thurow, *The Future of Capitalism: How Today's Economic Forces Shape Tomorrow's World* (New York: William Morrow, 1996), 130. Similar arguments in favor of convergence can be found in Kenichi Ohmae (ed.), *The Evolving Global Economy: Making Sense of the New World Order* (Boston: Harvard Business Review, 1995); id., *The Borderless World: Power and Strategy in the Interlinked Economy* (New York: Harper Perennial, 1991); and Robert Reich, *The Work of Nations* (New York: Knopf, 1991).

Among those who generally discount the claims of the convergence school are Michel Albert in his discussion of the neo-American versus Rhine models of capitalism in *Capitalism against Capitalism* (London: Whurr, 1993); Robert Wade in 'Globalization and its Limits: Reports of the

Death of the National Economy are Greatly Exaggerated,' in Suzanne Berger and Ronald Dore (eds.), *National Diversity and Global Capitalism* (Ithaca, NY: Cornell University Press, 1996), ch. 2; and Jeffrey A. Hart in his arguments concerning different 'state-societal arrangements' in Britain, France, Germany, Japan, and the United States in *Rival Capitalists: International Competitiveness in the United States, Japan and Western Europe* (Ithaca, NY: Cornell University Press, 1992).

For general overviews of recent debates concerning convergence theory see, in particular, the excellent contributions of Suzanne Berger, 'Introduction,' and Robert Boyer, 'The Convergence Hypothesis Revisited: Globalization but Still the Century of Nations?,' in Berger and Dore (eds.), *National Diversity and Global Capitalism*, 1–25, 29–59.

1

Approaching the Challenge

JAPANESE FDI first entered European markets in the late nineteenth century and established a number of enduring patterns, yet recent Japanese direct investments in the region have broken with these patterns. In terms of relevant political changes, the modern history of Japanese FDI in Europe breaks down into five principal periods. These changes represent either important shifts in government policies or major international political events which critically affected Japanese investment flows to Europe. Continuity rather than change best characterizes key features of Japanese FDI in Europe through most of its first century of development, but many characteristics of this investment have changed markedly in more recent times. This historical disjuncture helps define one important aspect of the larger European context, as officials in the region debated alternative policy approaches to the gathering Japanese Challenge.[1]

THE DEVELOPMENT OF JAPANESE FDI IN EUROPE

Origins

Japan's earliest direct investments in Europe began in the late nineteenth century, and were aimed primarily at facilitating bilateral trade flows. These flows proved critically important to Japan, which in its strategy to industrialize sought to import machinery and other advanced capital equipment from the West and export in exchange raw silk, and textiles and other relatively simple manufactured products, to this same region. Rather than America, Europe initially represented Japan's principal Western trading partner. Europe supplied a far greater proportion of Japanese imports than did its Atlantic counterpart for at least the four decades preceding World War I, for example, and Europe consumed a greater proportion of Japanese exports than did North America at least through the 1870s (see Figs. 1 and 2). The United Kingdom far outstripped other European countries as a source of Japanese imports, which comprised mainly manufacturing machinery and other capital goods, through World War I (and beyond) (see Fig. 3). Among European nations, France from the mid-1870s until 1914 was the largest recipient of Japanese exports, which comprised largely raw silk and silk products (see Fig. 4).

To facilitate this trade, Japanese enterprise set up European affiliates in at least four different commercial fields. Trading companies established local offices to import and sell Japanese goods in Europe, and to acquire European products and technology and export them to Japan. Unquestionably the most important Japanese trading firm in Europe during this period was Mitsui & Co., which in 1878 chose Paris as the site for its first branch office in the Western world.[2] Although Mitsui & Co. apparently judged that business did not warrant the continued operation of the Paris (or 1880-established Milan) office for long, the trading company did identify other European regions as sufficiently important to justify a local presence, and soon operated branch offices in London (established in 1880), Lyons (established in 1880, closed in 1881, and reopened in 1908), and Hamburg (1899) (see Table 1). Nor was Mitsui & Co. the only Japanese trading firm which directly invested in Europe during this period. Okura Gumi, for example, operated branch or subbranch offices in London and Hamburg after the (1904–5) Russo-Japanese War, and Nihon Menka established Menka Gesellschaft in Bremen, Germany, and set up branches in, or dispatched employees to, Liverpool, London, and Milan well before the start of World War I.[3]

In addition to trading companies, Japanese enterprise established European operations in at least three other main business lines to enhance bilateral trade. For example, the Yokohama Specie Bank (YSB; predecessor of the Bank of Tokyo), which was established in 1880, the very next year set up its first European representative office in London largely to provide foreign exchange, export and import financing, and other financial services related to such trade, and later established a Hamburg office as well.[4] In addition, the YSB's London branch served as a vital conduit of foreign capital, for through this branch the Bank marketed Japanese government-backed securities to European (principally British) investors.[5]

Japanese affiliates in Europe also facilitated trade through provi-

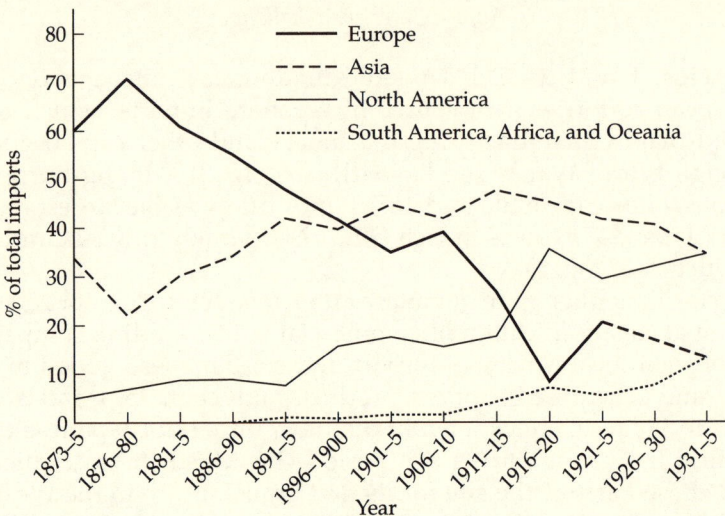

FIG. 1. Average annual shares of Japanese imports, by source region, 1873–1935

Source: Sugiyama Shinya, *Japan's Industrialization in the World Economy, 1859–1899: Export Trade and Overseas Competition* (London: Athlone Press, 1988), table A-2.

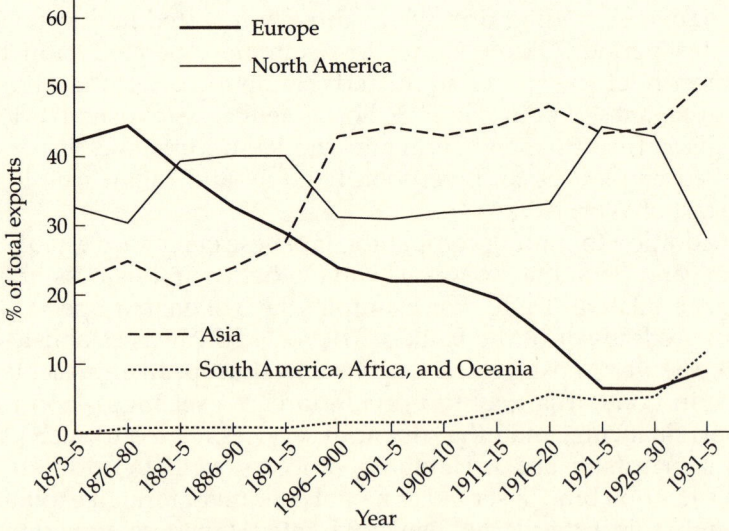

FIG. 2. Average annual shares of Japanese exports, by recipient region, 1873–1935

Source: As Fig. 1.

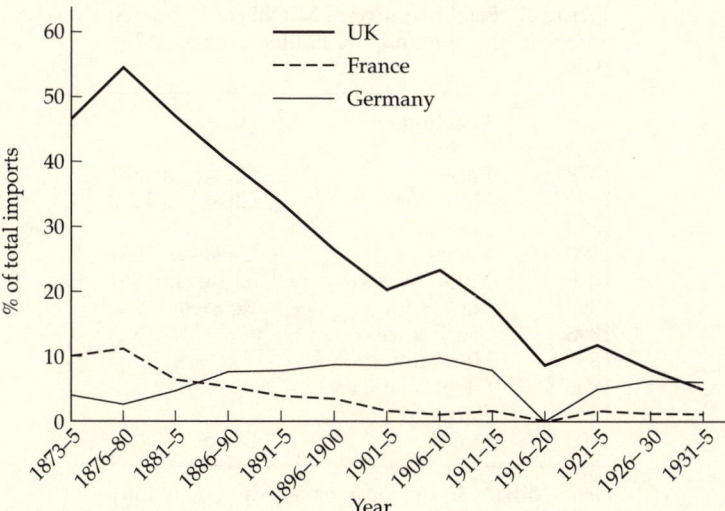

FIG. 3. Average annual shares of Japanese imports, by principal European sources, 1873–1935

Source: As Fig. 1.

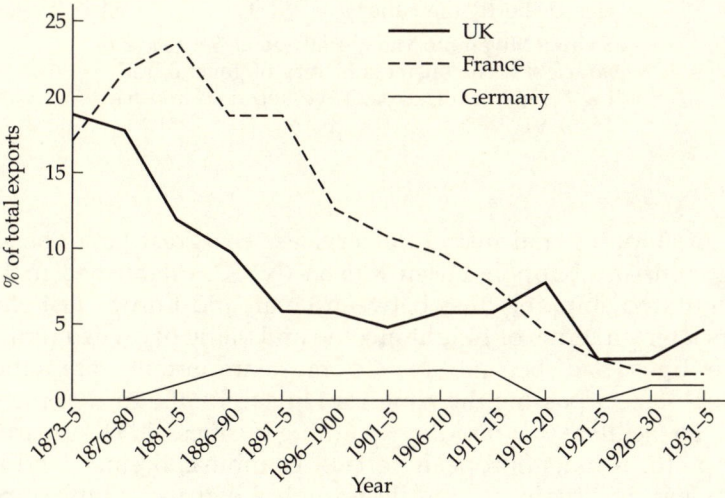

FIG. 4. Average annual shares of Japanese exports, by principal European recipients, 1873–1935

Source: As Fig. 1.

TABLE 1. Establishment of Mitsui & Co. branch offices in Europe and the United States, 1878–1908

Year	Location	Notes
1878	Paris	Closes in 1881
1879	New York	Closes in 1882
1880	London	
1880	Lyons	Closes in 1881
1880	Milan	Closes in 1881
1896	New York	Reopens
1898	San Francisco	
1899	Hamburg	
1906	Oklahoma City	
1907	Portland	
1908	Lyons	Reopens

Note: Mitsui & Co. also established a wholly owned subsidiary, Southern Products Company, in Houston, Texas in 1911. See Mitsui & Co., *The 100-Year History of Mitsui & Co., Ltd.* (Tokyo: Mitsui & Co., 1977), 50. Soon after its founding, this subsidiary apparently took over the functions of the Oklahoma City office, which closed shortly thereafter.

Source: Miyamoto Mataji et al. (eds.), *Sogo shosha no keieishi* (The business history of general trading companies) (Tokyo: Toyo keizai shinposha, 1976), 91.

sion of shipping and insurance services. The great Japanese shipping company Nippon Yusen Kaisha (NYK), established in 1885, inaugurated shipping lines between Japan and Europe just eleven years later. In terms of freight income and value of owned tonnage, these lines had become NYK's most important international routes—far surpassing the American lines—by the turn of the century. To facilitate this rapidly expanding business, NYK apparently set up offices in its European ports of Hamburg, Bremen, and Antwerp and, in Britain, in Middlesbrough, Liverpool, Southampton, and London.[6]

And the Tokio Marine Insurance Company, for its part, was the most important Japanese supplier of shipping and other insurance services principally to cover the transportation of goods between Japan and Europe during these years. Tokio Marine entrusted Mitsui & Co. agencies in Paris and London with representing its European interests in 1880, but later chose to create its own London office.[7] Already experiencing rapid growth through contract sales for accident insurance through this office, in 1898 Tokio Marine chose to expand its British-based activities to include international cargo insurance and other trade-related business. Several other Japanese insurance companies also operated London offices to conduct such business, although Tokio Marine clearly dominated the field.[8] Through trading company branches, financial services outlets, shipping offices and insurance agencies, European affiliates of Japanese-based enterprises promoted two-way trade vital to Japan's industrializing economy.

The intimate involvement of the Japanese government stands out as a particularly striking feature of the nation's earliest direct investments in Europe. Indeed, the government directly supported the European activities of each of the leading Japanese companies involved in these bilateral trade-facilitating activities. To NYK, for example, the Japanese authorities provided substantial subsidies to cover the costs of operating the European line.[9] For the YSB, the government initially provided one-third of the capital and determined appointments of the President and Vice President and, later, took effective control of the entire organization.[10] In Tokio Marine, the government initially held a substantial number of the firm's shares.[11] And for Mitsui & Co., the authorities provided subsidies and interest-free loans to encourage exports to Europe, and at one point even granted the trading company's Paris office the exclusive right to market silk manufactured in Japan's state-run spinning mills throughout France.[12]

Despite the relatively early entry of Japanese FDI in Europe, however, overall investment levels—together with the European impacts of such investment—remained extremely modest. Although detailed statistical figures do not exist, anecdotal and other evidence suggests that Japanese FDI in Europe before World War I was limited to the modest sums required to establish the kinds of service organizations outlined above.[13] And although the impacts of such investments surely were critical to Japan, these investments constituted only a tiny proportion of the FDI which entered any of the European countries in this period, and generally had little effect on the operation of these economies.[14] Reflecting this limited presence, European attitudes towards Japan and its local investments, to the extent that they even existed, generally were characterized by indifference, if not condescension. In this environment, European officials felt no need to craft specific policies to deal with these early Japanese entrants.

Inter-war Expansion (1914–1941)

Following a brief hiatus created by the start of World War I, Japanese firms generally expanded their investments in Europe before World War II. The outbreak of war in 1914 initially slowed Japan's trade with Europe.[15] As a result, the European operations of Japanese-based trading, finance, transportation, and insurance companies at first declined, and few new investments were undertaken. Instead, Japanese investors concentrated their efforts still further on other Asian markets, where they could partially fill the void created by the drop in the region's trade with Europe, and on the United States, which became an increasingly important alternative Western trading partner.[16]

Well before the end of World War I, however, trade with Europe once again increased, and Japanese trading firms and other companies took advantage of this renewed activity to expand their investments in Europe.[17] Indeed, compared with earlier years, evidence suggests that a far greater number of Japanese trading companies chose to set up offices in Europe between the two world wars. By the mid-1920s, for example, leading traders such as Nihon Menka, Mitsubishi Shoji, Suzuki Shoten, Iwai Shoten, Okura Shoji, Takashimaya Iida, and Ataka Shokai in addition to Mitsui & Co. had established branch offices in London alone.[18] Before World War II they were joined in London by Naniwa Boeki Shokai and Showa Menka.[19] Some of these same firms also operated offices elsewhere in Europe during this period, such as Mitsui & Co.'s French and German subsidiaries, and Mitsubishi Shoji's branches or offices in Berlin, Lyons, Marseilles, Paris, and Rome.[20]

Not only did the number of Japanese trading firms expand significantly in pre-World War II Europe, they also took on an increasing range of functions. Initially, such firms principally engaged in the bilateral import and export of a relatively small number of products such as machinery, textiles, and raw silk, and the transfer to Japan of various European technologies. In the inter-war period, however, these companies expanded the range of traded products to include coal, metal, produce, oils and fats, marine products, chemicals, and miscellaneous goods.[21] Moreover, an ever larger number of these firms engaged in third-country trade, such as Mitsui & Co.'s active trade in Indian jute, which the firm purchased from its Calcutta branch and sold to its London office.[22] And finally, the European operations of Japanese trading firms played increasingly important roles as sources of market intelligence in the United Kingdom, France, Germany, and elsewhere. Often, these European-based subsidiaries became the eyes and ears not only of Japanese business, but of the Japanese government as well.[23]

Other Japanese service organizations also expanded their European presence during the decades preceding World War II. The Mitsubishi Bank and, apparently, the Mitsui Bank as well, set up London branches in the inter-war era, for example, although the Sumitomo Bank lived up to its reputation—'The Yokohama Specie Bank aside, the Sumitomo Bank was the earliest [Japanese] bank to develop overseas,' according to common wisdom—by establishing its own London branch in 1918, which pre-dated these Mitsubishi and Mitsui operations.[24] The Yokohama Specie Bank, for its part, opened branches in Paris and Berlin (both in 1931) in addition to previously established offices in London and Hamburg.[25] And numerous Japanese shipping lines apparently set up agencies in Europe to support the expansion of their services to that region in the inter-war period.[26]

In the insurance industry, at least ten Japanese companies operated offices in pre-war Britain alone. In addition to Tokio Marine, these offices represented, among others, the Mitsubishi, Sumitomo, and Taisho interests.[27] Some of these London-based operations, such as Taisho Marine and Fire Insurance Company, developed rather extensive business relationships with numerous British reinsurance firms during this period.[28]

Despite these examples of increasing Japanese direct investment in inter-war Europe, however, available evidence suggests that the amounts of such investment remained quite small throughout the period. The few official Japanese statistics on foreign investment before World War II, for example, do not even mention the existence of Japanese FDI in Europe. Rather, these and other limited data emphasize the considerable build-up of such FDI in Asia primarily, and in the South Pacific, Hawaii, and North America secondarily.[29] It is therefore quite understandable that European governments did not establish policy frameworks to control or otherwise influence Japan's still limited direct presence in the region.

War- and Occupation-Induced Disruption (1941–1951)

The decade of war and occupation from 1941 generally froze and then erased the pre-war investments of Japanese companies in Europe. Like America, for example, Great Britain froze all Japanese assets in its territories months before Pearl Harbor. Many of Japan's European investments remained frozen or were transferred to native control in the Allied nations during the war, and the operations of Japanese firms virtually ceased to function in most of the other countries of Europe as well.[30] In Great Britain, the authorities ordered the freezing of Japanese assets on July 26, 1941, which led Japan to freeze British assets in its territory two days later.[31] The British government designated Japanese firms 'enemy' concerns on December 8, 1941, and shifted control of their assets to the official Custodian of Alien Property. In many cases, such as those of Mitsui & Co., Tokio Marine, NYK, and the YSB, the Board of Trade, under authority of the Trading with the Enemy Act of 1939, then appointed British nationals to act as 'controllers' of individual 'enemy' companies to oversee taxation and other matters.[32]

The German case constituted the one important exception to Europe's treatment of Japanese investment during World War II. In fact, rather than impound or appropriate Japan's direct investments in its territories, Axis partner Germany actively *encouraged* the growth of such investment. This policy of encouragement was formally adopted when the German and Japanese governments signed a bilateral economic treaty on January 20, 1943. 'Japan and Germany shall devote their total strength to promote economic interchange in every field between their respective countries,' read the first article of the Agreement between Japan and Germany Concerning Economic Cooperation. 'Each nation shall assist the other in procuring goods and establishing facilities in its domain, and the two nations shall furthermore engage in close and intimate technical cooperation.'[33] Despite this official policy, however, Japanese investments in Germany apparently remained quite small throughout the war years.[34]

Virtually from the start of the (1945–52) Allied Occupation of Japan, the Supreme Commander for the Allied Powers (SCAP) prohibited almost all transactions involving Japanese investment abroad by persons located in Japan.[35] Indeed, in September 1945 SCAP forbade the transfer of Japan's external assets belonging not only to Japanese corporations and financial institutions, but also to government agencies and private individuals. The Allied authorities then systematically inventoried these external assets.[36] In Europe and elsewhere, Japan's foreign investments remained blocked until the close of the Occupation. Investments made before or during World War II in general were controlled by the government of the territory in which they were located at the conclusion of hostilities, although some of these investments were liquidated (and others, principally located in Manchuria, were literally carried off by the Soviet military).[37]

At the signing of the Peace Treaty in September 1951, signatory countries apparently adopted a definitive policy towards the disposition of Japan's pre-war and wartime foreign investments and other external assets located within their territories. Under the terms of the Treaty, those nations which had been at war with Japan were allowed to confiscate and liquidate virtually all Japanese assets in their respective jurisdictions.[38] According to an internal British government report at the end of the Occupation, the British authorities chose to use proceeds from the sale of Japanese assets in their territory 'for the benefit of former prisoners-of-war and internees who suffered in Japanese hands.'[39] Yet, according to another internal government memorandum, many intended beneficiaries became deeply dissatisfied with the process, for 'Japanese assets [were] so small in relation to the claims against Japan.'[40] Japan's assets located in former Axis and wartime neutral countries apparently were transferred by Japan to the International Committee of the Red Cross, which sold them off. Proceeds from the sale of these assets, as in the British case, were later used to compensate certain former Allied prisoners of war.[41] In short, soon after the turn of the decade Japan had lost almost its entire range of foreign direct investments located in Europe (and elsewhere). And for the first time, European governments had enacted policies towards the local investments of Japanese business.

Under the circumstances of war and occupation, it is hardly surprising that Japanese direct investment in 1940s Europe remained extremely limited before its virtual elimination at the turn of the new decade. Indeed, evidence suggests that the vast majority of Japanese FDI during this period was located in nearby Asian territories, which, in the early part of the decade, were generally controlled by the Japanese government. Based on its own investigations, for example, SCAP calculated that no less than 93.69 per cent of all Japanese external assets were located in China, Manchuria, Korea, and Formosa (Taiwan) in August 1945; just 6.31 per cent reportedly were situated elsewhere at that time.[42] And the British government estimated that total Japanese assets of all types in Great Britain as of 1952 stood at less than £1 million.[43] A vast amount of anecdotal evidence supports these overall SCAP and British government figures.[44]

Post-war Resumption (1951–1971)

The Japanese government established a new era in the history of Japan's foreign direct investment in Europe towards the close of the Allied Occupation. Less than one year after the limited reopening of Japan to FDI from abroad, in 1951 the local authorities—increasingly independent of SCAP regulation—revoked the blanket ban on outward investment which had been operative throughout much of the 1940s.

Like their treatment of inward flows, however, Japanese officials carefully regulated all overseas investments through powers contained in the 1949 Foreign Exchange and Foreign Trade Control Law (FEFTCL). Specifically, the Ministry of Finance (MOF), often in concert with other interested agencies such as the Ministry of International Trade and Industry (MITI), carried out an 'individual examination' (*kobetsu shinsa*) of every potential Japanese direct investment abroad over roughly the next two decades, and denied requisite foreign exchange to those investment proposals which did not gain their approval. This the authorities accomplished by calling together a liaison conference of concerned ministries to deliberate the merits and demerits of each and every proposed case.[45]

Official motives and standards were not publicly clarified, but the pattern of decisions suggests the authorities' underlying intent. The government apparently instituted its control policy both to conserve scarce foreign exchange reserves and to prevent 'reverse imports' of manufactured products from Japanese affiliates abroad back to the home market. (The latter eventuality, it was feared, could damage smaller, less efficient Japanese producers without access to the advantages of overseas production.[46]) Specific screening criteria, however, varied by industry, were vaguely worded and often became subject to differing interpretations.[47] As we shall see, in practice the authorities approved limited numbers of direct investments in Europe generally by those domestic firms best positioned to enhance Japanese exports to European markets.

The verdict of the government's deliberations, however, generally affected more than an applicant's access to foreign exchange. In addition, those investments which did receive government approval often benefited from official support such as low-interest loans and special tax advantages. In short, through positive as well as negative measures the Japanese government played a critical role in the post-war development of Japan's FDI in Europe.[48]

Responding to these new—though still severely circumscribed—investment freedoms, numerous Japanese firms managed to gain the government's consent to invest directly in Europe during this era. Mimicking the pre-war investment pattern, many of these early post-war entrants were trading companies which set up wholly-owned subsidiaries. Mitsui & Co., the Mitsubishi Corporation (successor to Mitsubishi Shoji), Marubeni, C. Itoh, and other general trading firms established or re-established offices in Europe throughout the 1950s. The very first such office set up by a major trading firm was the Mitsui & Co. branch in London (1953), but official Japanese data suggest that the vast majority of such trading offices in the 1950s were located in West Germany rather than England (see Table 2). The Mitsubishi Corporation apparently became the first important Japanese direct investor in post-war France when, in 1960, it established a limited corporation in Paris to import and export metals and other goods. Mitsubishi invested 94 per cent of the capital, and French interests committed the remainder.[49]

In addition, numerous trading firms established joint ventures in Europe principally during the 1960s, often investing with Japanese manufacturers to market the latter's products in European countries. By the end of that decade, for example, Marubeni had established joint ventures with Japanese firms to market chemicals in West Germany (Sekisui Chemical GmbH; set up in 1962) as well as electrical goods in England (Sanyo Marubeni [UK] Ltd.; 1969). In addition, Marubeni joint ventured with European capital to create

TABLE 2. Japanese FDI in Europe, by firm and host country, 1951–1961 (notifications basis)

Japanese parent	European affiliate	Date	Industry	Location
Belgium				
Marubeni Iida	Société Belge Marubeni-Iida SPRL	1957	Trading	Brussels
England				
Mitsui & Co.	Mitsui & Co., Ltd., London	1953	Trading	London
Kawasaki Steamship	Kawasaki SS Co. (London)	1956	Trading	London
Takaraisu Sales	Belmont Chairs (London), Ltd.	1959	Trading	London
France				
Mitsubishi Corp.	Mitsubishi France	1960	Trading	Paris
Germany				
Mitsubishi Corp.	Deutsche Mitsubishi	1955	Trading	Düsseldorf
Mitsui & Co.	Deutsche Bussan	1955	Trading	Hamburg
Marubeni Iida	Marubeni Iida GmbH	1955	Trading	Hamburg
Toyo Menka	Toyo Menka GmbH	1956	Trading	Hamburg
Gosho	Gosho GmbH	1956	Trading	Hamburg
C. Itoh & Co.	C. Itoh & Co.	1956	Trading	Hamburg
Nissho	Deutsche Nissho Import & Export GmbH	1956	Trading	Hamburg
Okura Trading	Okura Trading Co., GmbH	1957	Trading	Düsseldorf
Kanematsu	F. Kanematsu & Co., GmbH	1957	Trading	Hamburg
Atake Industries	Deutsche Atake GmbH	1957	Trading	Hamburg
Sumitomo Trading	Deutsche Sumitomo Export & Import, GmbH	1958	Trading	Düsseldorf

Far East Trading	Far East Mercantile, GmbH	1958	Trading	Frankfurt
Nichimen Industries	Deutsche Nichimen, GmbH	1959	Trading	Hamburg
Kinoshita Trading	Deutsche Kinoshita, GmbH	1959	Trading	Düsseldorf
Osaka Trade Association	UTO Import & Export GmbH	1960	Trading	Hamburg
Momoi Textile	Deutsche Momoi Co. GmbH	1960	Trading	Hamburg
Iwai Industries	Iwai & Co., GmbH	1961	Trading	Düsseldorf
Honda Giken Industries	European Honda Motor, GmbH	1961	Trading	Hamburg
Ireland				
Brother International	Brother International Corp. (Europe)	1958	Trading	Dublin
Sony	Sony Ltd. (Shannon)	1959	Machinery	Shannon
Toyo Menka Feather Working Machine	Tomen (Ireland) Ltd.	1960	Machinery	Dublin
Portugal				
Mitsui & Co. Shinetsu Chemical Industries	União Electrica Portuguesa SARL	1960	Other	Porto
Switzerland				
Chugai Pharmaceutical	Yoroppa Chugai	1958	Trading	Zurich
Taiyo Fishery Industries	Taiyo & Suisse & ARL	1960	Trading	Geneva
Sony	Sony Overseas SA	1960	Trading	Zug

Note: This listing does not include banks and insurance companies.

Source: Bank of Japan.

local companies such as Promotores de Inversiones, SA in Spain (1964).[50] Mitsui & Co. also went beyond mere investments in its own trading branches to participate in a wide range of joint ventures throughout Europe in the 1960s.

A limited number of Japanese banks also gained MOF approval and chose to invest. Fuji Bank and Teikoku Bank, in addition to the Bank of Tokyo, managed to establish representative offices in London by September 1952. A number of other Japanese banks also sought permission to set up offices in London at the end of the Occupation, but MOF initially permitted them to start business only in New York.[51] In 1956, however, the Ministry modified its position to allow the Mitsubishi Bank and the Sumitomo Bank to resume business in London.[52]

Yet trading companies and banks were not the only Japanese firms which directly invested in post-war Europe. In addition, from about 1960 an increasing number of Japan's major manufacturers began to set up local operations on their own principally to distribute and sell their wares directly to European consumers. Electronics producers were among the first to do so. Among this group Sony apparently was the pioneer, for it managed to establish not only the first post-war direct investment in Europe by a Japanese electronics maker, but also the first post-war direct *manufacturing* investment in Europe by *any* major Japanese corporation. This Sony accomplished when in 1959 it set up a small plant in Shannon, Ireland, to manufacture transistor radios.[53] To support the company's European efforts and take advantage of local tax laws, Sony then established a regional office in Zug, Switzerland (Sony Overseas, SA), the following year.[54] Sony steadily built up its European presence, gradually shifting from local sales agents to wholly Sony-owned marketing operations (in addition to limited production facilities) during the 1960s.[55] Matsushita soon followed Sony's lead, creating sales subsidiaries for radios, televisions, tape recorders, and other products in West Germany (1962) and France (1968).[56]

Japanese automobile makers also began their move into Europe during the 1960s. Toyota, for example, established marketing organizations in some of its principal European markets starting early in the decade. The first such organization Toyota set up in Denmark (1963), followed by the creation of similar operations in the Netherlands (1964), Finland (1964), the United Kingdom (1965), Belgium (1966), Switzerland (1966), Portugal (1968), and Sweden

(1968).[57] Nissan established similar sales operations in Europe during these same years, followed by the company's first European assembly arrangement—the establishment of Entreposto Comercial Veiculos e Macquinas, SA, a Nissan-created and wholly-owned importer of knocked down commercial vehicle kits, with assembly entrusted to the locally-owned Entreposto Comercial de Automoveis—in Portugal in July 1968.[58] Toyota set up its own importing and assembly operation to produce commercial vehicles in Portugal—in Toyota's case, in concert with the local firm Salvador Caetano IMVT, SA—just three months later.[59] Both of these Japanese motor vehicle producers had been preceded in Europe, however, by Honda, which in 1961 had created a European regional sales office in Hamburg, West Germany (European Honda Motor GmbH), followed by a British sales branch in London in 1962, both principally to support its burgeoning motorcycle sales.[60]

Despite these and other examples of Japanese FDI in post-war Europe, however, the quantity and impact of such investment remained quite limited. According to official Japanese statistics, for example, Japan's total FDI outflows to Europe from 1951 to 1970 amounted to just $636 million.[61] As in earlier periods, these modest amounts of investment remained concentrated primarily in the larger European markets such as the United Kingdom, West Germany, and France. Yet such investments seem to have created little impact on any of these European economies, or on policymakers based there.

Growth and Diversification (1971–Present)

Japanese direct investment in Europe entered a new era in the early 1970s, and once again the Japanese government played a critical role in fostering the transition. Roughly paralleling its progressive liberalization of controls over *inward* direct investment, from 1969 the government inaugurated a five-stage process to deregulate controls over *outward* direct investment as well (see Table 3).[62] Although the final stage of this process was not implemented until 1978, the government undertook its critical third-stage liberalization in late 1971. From that time onward, with few exceptions the Ministry of Finance automatically validated proposals by Japanese companies to establish greenfield investments abroad without financial limit. This key change in government policy—essentially

TABLE 3. Liberalization of Japanese outward foreign direct investment, 1969–1978

Stage	Date	Chief measures
First liberalization	Oct. 1, 1969	Automatic validation for [greenfield] FDI: up to $200,000.
		[Conditions for] automatic validation for investments which augment the capital of foreign juridical persons: Japanese capital must constitute 25% or more of the total, and there must be at least one full-time manager sent from Japan.
		Exceptions to the above (designated industries and so forth): (1) the fisheries industry as reflected in international fisheries treaties; (2) the fisheries industry as designated in the Fisheries Industry Law or as approved by the Minister of Agriculture and Forestry; (3) the pearl farming industry; (4) the banking and securities industries; (5) cases which may cause problems in terms of international cooperation or foreign affairs; (6) cases which may create a very negative effect on the Japanese economy; (7) direct investments by banks or securities companies.
Second liberalization	Sept. 1, 1970	Automatic validation for [greenfield] FDI: up to $1 million.
		[Conditions for] automatic validation for investments which augment the capital of foreign juridical persons: (1) Japanese capital must constitute 50% or more of the total capital of the foreign juridical person; (2) the Japanese capital ratio is 25% or more but less than 50% and there is more than one full-time manager sent from Japan. Exceptions to the above (designated industries and so forth): [(1), (3)–(7): same as above]; (2) the fisheries industry as designated in the Fisheries Industry Law.
Third liberalization	July 1, 1971	Automatic validation for [greenfield] FDI: No financial limit.
		[Conditions for] automatic validation for investments which augment the capital of foreign juridical persons: (1) the Japanese capital ratio must constitute 25% or more of the total capital; (2) the Japanese capital ratio is 10% or more but less than 25%, and it is a

TABLE 3. *Continued*

Stage	Date	Chief measures
		foreign juridical which is characterized by one of the following: (*a*) Japanese managers; (*b*) manufacturing technology assistance; (*c*) purchases basic materials; (*d*) purchases manufactured products and so forth; (*e*) capital subsidies; (*f*) tie-up through a contract for a general agent's office.
		Exceptions to the above (designated industries and so forth): [same as above].
Fourth liberalization	June 8, 1972	Automatic validation for [greenfield] FDI: No financial limit.
		[Conditions for] automatic validation for investments which augment the capital of foreign juridical persons: (1) [same as above]; (2) if the Japanese capital ratio is below 25% and it is a foreign juridical person which is characterized by one of the following: [(*a*)–(*f*): same as above]; (*g*) in addition, there is a permanent economic relationship with the industry into which the capital will be invested.
		Exceptions to the above (designated industries and so forth): [same as above].
Fifth liberalization	Apr. 1, 1978	Automatic validation for [greenfield] FDI: No financial limit.
		[Conditions for] automatic validation for investments which augment the capital of foreign juridical persons: (1) [same as above]; (2) [same as above]. Note: acquisition of foreign securities is now placed under a notification system with the Bank of Japan. (However, the below-enumerated items are subject to a system of compulsory validation.)
		Exceptions to the above (designated industries and so forth): [(1)–(4), (7): same as above]; (5) the manufacture of textile products; (6) manufacturing industries engaged in the production of weapons and narcotics, etc.; (8) investment in South Africa or Namibia.

Note: All dollar amounts in US dollars.

Source: *Zaisei kinyu tokei geppo*, 452 (Dec. 1989), 3–6.

motivated not only by rising balance of payments surpluses but also by increasing pressures from Japanese business—created important new opportunities for domestic firms to invest abroad without precedent in the post-war period.[63]

Japanese FDI in Europe began to increase significantly from the early 1970s in response to these changes in government policies as well as numerous economic and other political developments. Shortly after the turn of the decade, for example, the appreciation of the yen, a rise in real domestic wages, and the prospect of greater competition at home as controls over inward direct investment eased all created powerful motivations for Japanese firms to directly invest abroad.[64] Indeed, the year 1972 often is referred to metaphorically as the 'gannen' of Japanese foreign direct investment—the term 'gannen' signifies the first year of a new imperial reign—for beginning that year Japanese FDI grew considerably as compared to earlier periods. Beginning in the mid-1980s, however, major new increases in the value of the yen, growing fears of European protectionism as the 1992 EC unification program progressed, and other factors all combined to produce far greater pressures for Japanese business to invest in the Community. These and other pressures led to dramatic surges in Japanese FDI in Europe beginning, as noted above, in the latter half of the 1980s.[65]

As in earlier periods, service-sector enterprises accounted for a substantial part of the increase in Japanese FDI to Europe during these years, although the relative importance of at least one major group of such Japanese enterprises changed significantly. Financial services firms established or expanded their direct investments in Europe from the 1970s. Japanese banks, for example, began to follow the growing numbers of their customers who invested in Europe, and by the late 1970s many such banks operated subsidiaries, branches, and offices in London, Frankfurt, Düsseldorf, Brussels, and elsewhere in the region.[66] Major investors in Europe by that time included the Bank of Tokyo, and the Dai Ichi Kangyo, Fuji, Sumitomo, Mitsubishi, Sanwa, and Mitsui Banks.[67] The large Japanese securities firms also established operations in Europe during these years. The 'Big Four' securities houses all set up offices in London at the start of this period—Nikko and Yamaichi in 1971, followed by Nomura and Daiwa in 1972—together with most other major firms in the securities industry by the end of the decade. Moreover, all or most of the 'Big Four' also created establishments in Paris, Frankfurt, and Amsterdam during these same years.[68] Numerous Japanese insurance companies similarly inaugurated or increased their European investments.

The Japanese government's 1980 revision of the Foreign Exchange and Foreign Trade Control Law encouraged many of these same financial services firms substantially to augment their presence in Europe.[69] Largely exempted from the capital liberalization process begun in 1969, Japan's financial services industry now invested in the UK and on the Continent still more aggressively. Major Japanese bank investments following the 1980 liberalization included Fuji Bank's 1982 buyout of its erstwhile equal partnership joint venture with Kleinwort Benson in Fuji International Finance Bank (London), the Long-Term Credit Bank of Japan's 1983 acquisition of full ownership in the Nippon European Bank (Brussels), and Sumitomo Bank's 1984 majority acquisition of Banca del Gottardo (Zurich).[70] These and other such investments were followed in part by bank acquisitions in southern Europe in the latter half of the decade, apparently to diffuse the Japanese presence to a wider number of European countries.[71] Japan's securities houses and insurance companies also increased their European direct investments especially from the middle of the decade.[72]

There are indications that, at least in relative terms, the historically important investment roles of the general trading companies (*sogo shosha*) may, however, have declined during this era. Following a brief burst of direct investment activity by the *sogo shosha* in Europe following the Japanese government's liberalization of outward FDI in the early 1970s, the number of their new investments declined dramatically thereafter. Indeed, the top nine general trading companies participated in just four new direct investments throughout Europe in 1977 and 1978, and none at all from 1979 through 1982.[73] Other data similarly suggest that, as compared with other Japanese investors, the activities of these firms in Europe became less significant. During the period 1978–81, for example, seven of the nine *sogo shosha* reported absolute *declines* in employment at their European-based trading subsidiaries. And at least one study indicates that these traders reduced their investments in sales companies and manufacturing firms in Europe during the late 1970s.[74] Nonetheless, the *sogo shosha* continued to play important roles in Europe as facilitators of trade and other economic activities throughout the 1970s, 1980s, and beyond.[75]

Similar to the record of many financial services firms, from the early 1970s Japanese manufacturing companies also began significantly to increase their direct investments in Europe. Many such investments took the form of importing, sales, and service organizations which bypassed the traditional role of the general trading company. Matsushita Electric, for example, continued its earlier build-up of European-based sales subsidiaries by establishing wholly-owned affiliates in virtually every large and even many smaller European markets during the 1970s and early 1980s.[76] Toyota added to its earlier network of European sales affiliates by setting up marketing organizations in Austria, France, Ireland, Italy, Germany, Greece, Norway, and Spain between 1970 and 1987.[77] Numerous other Japanese manufacturers pursued similar investment strategies in Europe from the early 1970s.

At the same time, and particularly during the latter half of the 1980s, large numbers of Japanese producers chose to establish assembly or manufacturing operations in Europe. The official Invest in Britain Bureau, for example, calculated that from 1972 though 1991 major Japanese companies established some 158 manufacturing subsidiaries in the UK, with the vast majority occurring after 1985.[78] And in France, the functionally equivalent public agency DATAR estimated that Japanese firms had established 43 local manufacturing concerns between 1970 and 1984, but some 101 such affiliates between 1985 and 1990.[79]

Electronics and automobile firms both numbered significantly among the range of Japanese manufacturing investors in Europe during this period. In the electronics industry, for example, virtually all of the major Japanese producers created or expanded their local manufacturing bases. Indeed, in this era Panasonic (Matsushita) alone established sixteen manufacturing companies in diverse locations within Europe to produce everything from batteries (Belgium, in a joint venture with Philips; 1970), to vacuum cleaners, VCRs, and hi-fis (Spain; 1973), to passive electronic components (in a joint venture with Siemens, headquartered in Germany; 1989).[80] Yet Panasonic was hardly alone: Hitachi, JVC, Mitsubishi Electric, NEC, Sanyo, Sharp, Sony, and Toshiba all had significant manufacturing investments in the European electronics industry by the end of the 1980s.

Japanese automobile companies also established assembly and manufacturing operations in Europe beginning in the early 1970s.

In 1972, for example, Toyota acquired a 27 per cent stake in Salvador Caetano, the Portuguese company to which it had heretofore consigned assembly of vehicles imported by a wholly Toyota-owned subsidiary (see above).[81] Indeed, Hino, Honda, Isuzu, Mitsubishi Motors, Nissan, and Toyo Kogyo (now Mazda) as well as Toyota all had established assembly operations in Europe by 1977—yet by that date not one had begun full-scale manufacturing in the region. These assembly operations were all located in Greece, Portugal, and Ireland, apparently to take advantage of low labor costs within the unifying European Community. This pattern contrasted with that of the American 'Big Three,' which by this date had established comprehensive manufacturing plants as well as assembly operations in a number of the higher-wage European countries (see Table 4).[82] Yet this situation changed dramatically beginning in the mid-1980s, from which time many of Japan's leading automakers began to commit substantial resources to invest directly in European manufacturing plants (see Chapter 2).[83]

These and other investments vastly expanded Japan's FDI presence in Europe. Indeed, as compared to the relatively small amounts of such FDI in previous decades, from the 1970s the growth rate of Japanese direct investment in Europe increased markedly, and, as noted above, beginning in the mid-1980s at truly dramatic rates. MOF data indicate that this investment grew more than sixfold between 1971 and 1980, for example, and more than tenfold between 1981 and 1990.[84] Recent trends in Japanese FDI to Europe are also striking when compared with trends to other major recipient regions. Beginning in 1984, for example, Japanese direct investment flows to Europe exceeded those to Asia on a sustained basis for the first time in history.[85] And although annual Japanese FDI outflows as well as accumulated direct investments in the United States still exceed such investments in Europe, the difference between the proportion of total Japanese FDI flowing to America versus Europe declined steadily as completion of the 1992 program approached.[86] In short, from numerous perspectives the two decades from 1971 witnessed a huge and unprecedented build-up of Japanese direct investment in Europe. This build-up led not only to a new geographic pattern of distribution within Europe and to major new impacts on Europe, but also, as discussed below, to major European policy initiatives in response.

TABLE 4. Automobile assembly and manufacturing plants in Europe: Japanese and American producers (1977)

	UK	France	W. Germany	Belgium	Switzerland	Netherlands	Denmark	Spain	Greece	Portugal	Ireland
Japanese producers											
Nissan										A	A
Toyota									A	A	A
Toyo kogyo (now Mazda)									A	A	A
Mitsubishi Motors										A	
Isuzu									A		
Honda										A	
Hino									A	A	A
American producers											
GM	M		M	A	A		A				
Ford	M		M	A		A	A			A	A
Chrysler	M	M		A	A	A		M	A	A	A

Notes: 'A' denotes assembly plant; 'M' denotes full manufacturing plant.

Source: Adapted from Fujii Mitsuo et al. (eds.), *Nihon takokuseki kigyo no shiteki tenkai* (The historical development of Japanese multinational enterprise), ii. 166.

CONTINUITY AND CHANGE

The development of Japanese direct investment in Europe exhibits at least eight striking continuities which generally characterize the first century or so of this development. Unlike this preceding century, however, beginning in the early 1970s—but often particularly beginning in the mid-1980s—new features of this investment reveal striking contrasts with the longer-term historical pattern. In this section, we shall consider each of these long-term continuities together with the significance of more recent changes.

Investment Levels

One of the most striking features of Japanese direct investment in Europe from its beginnings in the late nineteenth century through the 1960s is its paucity. During the decades before World War II, for example, available evidence suggests that the overall quantities of FDI which entered Europe were very small. These modest amounts then declined during World War II, and by the end of the Allied Occupation the systematic elimination of Japan's pre-war FDI in Europe had virtually wiped the slate clean. Nor did renewed independence usher in a period of large-scale investment in Europe, for during the 1950s and 1960s the Japanese government severely restricted FDI outflows to the region.

In contrast to the meager amounts of Japanese FDI which entered Europe during its nearly first century of development, however, comparatively great amounts of such investment have accumulated there in more recent times. The Japanese government's capital liberalization program begun in 1969 marked a watershed in the nation's regulation of investment outflows, and in succeeding years this liberalization program together with powerful economic as well as other political forces led to substantial increases in the nation's direct investments in Europe. As a result, Japanese FDI in Europe expanded significantly from about 1970 to the mid-1980s, and then increased dramatically during the latter half of the 1980s.

Sectoral Composition

A pronounced bias towards direct investment in the service sector constitutes a second major continuity in the historical development of Japanese FDI in Europe. From Japan's very first investments in the 1870s down to the present, firms in such industries as trade, banking, and insurance have been among the most active Japanese direct investors in the region. The relative importance of specific industries within the service sector has varied over time, yet the general predominance of services has not.

Although the sectoral breakdown of more recent Japanese direct investments in Europe still clearly favors the service sector, beginning in the early 1970s and then particularly from the mid-1980s an increasing range of companies in other sectors also invested there. Indeed, although by the early 1990s most accumulated Japanese FDI in Europe remained in services, direct investments in the machinery, chemical, and other manufacturing industries, together with FDI in other non-service fields such as real estate and mining, by then accounted for a substantial proportion of accumulated Japanese direct investment in the region.

Location

From its first appearance in modern Europe and for many decades thereafter, Japanese direct investment was highly concentrated in a few major European markets. In fact, the record of Mitsui & Co.'s establishment of branch offices in nineteenth-century Europe—all but one of which were located in England, France, or Germany—reflects a pattern of Japanese investments in the region which endured for practically a century. That pattern not only held for trading companies, but also for banking, insurance, and many other types of direct investments as well.

In more recent times, however, there has been a shift in Japanese FDI in Europe from geographical concentration to geographical dispersion. In contrast to the pre-war anecdotal evidence and the post-war statistical evidence, both of which point up the high concentration of Japanese investment in just a few of the principal European economies, from the 1970s substantial amounts of Japanese FDI flowed to a far wider range of countries in the region. Indeed, as noted above, this change led to a major locational redistribution of such investment which, by 1993, had rendered the Netherlands (largely for tax and other legal reasons) the second-ranking recipient of accumulated stocks of Japanese FDI in Europe, and which raised measurably the levels of such FDI in Spain, Belgium, and Italy (for economic but also political reasons).[87]

Motivation

Yet another clear historical continuity in the development of Japanese FDI in Europe until the recent past has been the underlying motivation to invest: from the earliest investments in the 1870s and for many decades thereafter, Japanese investors sought principally to enhance bilateral trade flows. In the pre-war period Japanese investors in the trade, shipping, banking, and insurance sectors generally sought to facilitate trade flows in both directions, and in the post-war era these investors principally concentrated on increasing Japanese exports to Europe. Yet at both times trade enhancement was the central motive.

Here again, however, the record of more recent years contrasts significantly with this longer-term historical pattern. Although much Japanese FDI in Europe still aimed at facilitating bilateral trade, more recently an increasing amount of such investment rather aimed at defending or enhancing European market share through the local provision of goods and services through European-based assembly, manufacturing, and other investments. Threats or perceived threats of European protectionism in the approach to market unification contributed powerfully to the increasing importance of this latter motive.[88]

Role of General Trading Companies

Over the course of the almost 120 years that Japan's general trading companies have operated in Europe, they have fulfilled at least four critically important functions. First, the general traders facilitated exports of Japanese products to Europe and imports of European products to Japan. Second, these firms transferred numerous European technologies to Japanese industry. Third, many of these same companies became information sources for Japanese business and government concerning economic, political, and other conditions in Europe. And fourth, principally during the post-war period the *sogo shosha* acted as joint venture partners with both Japanese and local manufacturing companies to expand their

European-based activities. Indeed, for many years the general traders constituted the largest single category of Japanese direct investors in Europe.[89]

In contrast to this long-standing importance of the *sogo shosha*,
however, in more recent times the relative significance of the general trading companies as investors in Europe has apparently declined. Although these firms still play important roles in bilateral
(and, indeed, multilateral) economic ties, since at least the mid-
1970s Japanese manufacturing companies in particular have begun
to invest directly in and otherwise transact economically with the
markets of Europe without the same degree of involvement by the
general traders common in years past. The large manufacturing
investments of Japanese automobile companies in the United Kingdom beginning in the 1980s provide only a few of the more recent
and vivid examples of this longer-term trend.

Role of the Japanese Government

From Japan's earliest direct investments in Europe and for many
decades thereafter, the Japanese government participated as an intimate and often highly influential player. One key government role
was to provide various types of assistance to Japanese investors in
Europe. This assistance dates back to the nineteenth century, and
includes capital participation, subsidies, low-interest loans, and
preferential or exclusive rights to market goods produced in Japan
by government-owned factories to select European markets
through local affiliates. Another central government role was to
control the types and amounts of Japanese FDI which entered Europe. In the post-World War II period, most notably, the government strictly regulated investment outflows to Europe and other
regions, and both before and after World War II the authorities
managed to influence Japan's direct investments in Europe by de-
nying assistance to some potential investors even as they granted
help to others.

After completion of the capital liberalization program in the
1970s, however, the role of the Japanese government became much
less important. In fact, as early as 1971 the authorities had removed
many of the key public controls on outward direct investments
which had operated for the previous two decades. And by 1980,
following revision of the Foreign Exchange and Foreign Trade Con-

trol Law, the government greatly eased regulations governing the external investments of numerous types of Japanese financial institutions, which had been largely exempted from earlier decontrol measures. These important changes do not mean, of course, that government no longer had any bearing on Japan's FDI in Europe. For one thing, certain Japanese public agencies still provide financial assistance such as low-interest loans to select Japanese investors in Europe. Far more importantly, as we shall see, *European-based* public agencies in recent years acted to influence greatly the character of Japan's direct investment in the area.

European Impacts

The extremely modest impacts of Japanese direct investment on the economies of Europe constitute yet another long-term continuity in the development of Japan's FDI in the region. It is true that, at certain periods and in certain specific industries, the impacts of such investment have been rather considerable. Japanese investments in the Lyons-based French silk trade before World War II stand out as one important historical case in point, as does the role played by the YSB's London branch in holding (and shifting) Japanese government balances at times so 'exceptionally large' that they caused significant 'disturbances' on the London money markets, especially in the late 1890s and early 1900s.[90] Yet such cases constitute the exception rather than the rule, and although Japanese FDI in Europe often had a great impact on the *Japanese* economy, the reverse was rarely true.

Yet here again the decades-old pattern was overturned, for especially from the mid-1980s the impacts of Japanese FDI in Europe became highly significant in a number of important sectors. The growth of Japanese investments in the automobile and electronics industries, to name just two of the more obvious examples, greatly influenced the competitive positions of many European-based producers, led to important technology flows in both directions, and significantly affected Europe's trade patterns as well. Japan's investments in the European financial services and real estate sectors also created important impacts, both economic and psychological. And, as we shall see, many of these same investments created important *political* effects, with regard to relations both between Japan and Europe and between individual European states.

European Attitudes

Finally, European attitudes of indifference or even condescension towards Japan's direct investments in Europe endured for many decades from the first such investments in the 1870s. The extremely limited amounts of Japanese FDI in pre-war Europe undoubtedly encouraged such attitudes, as did Japan's status as a late industrial developer. Increased Japanese penetration during World War I of Asian markets previously supplied by European producers, conflicts between British and Japanese textile makers between the two world wars, and the pronounced rise of Japanese military and industrial power in the 1930s at times seriously challenged these long-held views, yet wartime defeat and subsequent occupation encouraged their return.[91]

Beginning in the early 1970s but especially after the mid-1980s, European attitudes changed quite markedly. Although attitudes clearly differed by country and otherwise, as EC unification approached European business and government leaders and often the general public as well devoted far more attention to foreign direct investment and other types of economic interactions with Japan. In many cases this interest turned into preoccupation and even outright fear, as suggested by some leading figures in France and elsewhere during these latter years.[92] Governments, in turn, would soon respond.

EUROPE, AMERICA, AND THE HISTORICAL DEVELOPMENT OF JAPANESE FDI

The development of Japanese direct investment in Europe exhibits striking continuities but also important changes. Many aspects of Japanese direct investment in modern Europe remained virtually constant from the late nineteenth century through the mid- to late twentieth century. As the foregoing analysis has shown, important elements of continuity during this period include investment levels, sectoral composition, location, motivation, the role of the general trading companies, the role of the Japanese government, European impacts, and European attitudes. There are exceptional examples of discontinuities for most of these categories, yet the overall historical pattern is clear.

Starting in the 1970s but far more pronounced during the latter half of the 1980s, however, the character of Japanese FDI in Europe underwent a number of profound changes. Investment levels surged far beyond the trajectory suggested by earlier trends, an increasing number of Japanese firms undertook direct manufacturing investments in the region, there developed a tendency towards greater geographical dispersion of this investment, and the overriding motivation shifted from trade creation to defense and enhancement of European market share through local value-added activities. Nor were these the only significant changes. In addition, later trends suggested far less significant roles for both the general trading companies and the Japanese government, growing Japanese FDI impacts on the economies of Europe, and a transformation in European attitudes from apathy to interest and, among some, to fear. As we shall see, these new attitudes in turn would encourage European officials to craft multifarious policies specifically designed to confront Japan's direct economic presence in the region.

Although this historical disjuncture in the development of Japanese FDI in Europe created an important contextual element as Europe contemplated its response to the Japanese Challenge, it was an experience largely shared by the Americans as well. Indeed, the similarities between the development of Japanese FDI in Europe and America are striking.[93] With respect to motivation, as in Europe the Japanese historically invested directly in the United States to support bilateral trade flows and inflows to Japan of foreign technology.[94] And similar to the European experience, so, too, in the American case Japanese firms in more recent years had become increasingly motivated to invest rather to defend or enhance local market share. Related to this changed motivation and again like Europe, Japanese FDI in America for decades was heavily concentrated in the service sector.[95] Yet since the 1970s and, in particular, the 1980s, greater proportions of this investment entered the US manufacturing and other sectors in addition to services.[96] And, just as in Europe, in America as well Japanese investors increasingly chose to disperse the locations of their investments from a few critical markets (such as those in New York and California in the US case) to a much wider range of locales.

There are, however, still more significant parallels between the historical development of Japanese FDI in Europe and America. US

Commerce Department data suggest, for example, that, just as in Europe, overall quantities of Japanese FDI in the United States were extremely limited both before World War II and for many years thereafter. Indeed, these data suggest that such investments generally accounted for less than 2 per cent of total FDI stocks in America through the early 1970s. Yet, similar to Europe, Japanese FDI surged into the United States in subsequent years—and particularly during the latter half of the 1980s—which vastly increased Japan's share of total FDI stocks in America.[97] This rapid rise of Japanese FDI after decades of only minimal investment greatly increased the economic impact of such investment in the United States, as it did in Europe. And this growing impact—together with, in the American case, highly sensationalized accounts of investments including the Mitsubishi Real Estate acquisition of a controlling interest in Rockefeller Center and the Sony acquisition of Columbia Pictures—in turn helped explain the heightened concern among many US as well as European policymakers over the ultimate implications of Japanese FDI for their respective recipient economies. Such concern set the stage for ensuing debates in both regions over the growing Japanese Challenge.

NOTES

1. Portions of this chapter, in an earlier version, were published in Mark Mason, 'The Origins and Evolution of Japanese Direct Investment in Europe,' *Business History Review*, 66 (Summer 1992), 435–74 and id., 'Historical Perspectives on Japanese Direct Investment in Europe,' in Mark Mason and Dennis Encarnation (eds.), *Does Ownership Matter? Japanese Multinationals in Europe* (Oxford: Oxford University Press, 1994), ch. 1.

2. In 1881, just three years after its establishment, however, the Paris branch was closed. See Togai Yoshio, 'Saisho ni shutsugen shita sogo shosha: Mitsui Bussan' (The first general trading company to move abroad: Mitsui & Co.), in Miyamoto Mataji et al. (eds.), *Sogo shosha no keieishi* (The business history of general trading companies) (Tokyo: Toyo keizai shinposha, 1976), 91.

3. Yamazaki Hiroaki, 'The Logic of the Formation of General Trading Companies in Japan,' in Yonekawa Shinichi and Yoshihara Hideki (eds.), *Business History of General Trading Companies* (Tokyo: University of Tokyo Press,

1987), 53; and Kawabe Nobuo, 'Development of Overseas Operations by General Trading Companies, 1868–1945,' in Yonekawa Shoichiro and Yoshihara Hideki (eds.), *Business History of General Trading Companies* (Tokyo: Tokyo University Press, 1987), 77.

4. Hijikata Susumu, *Yokohama shokin ginko* (The Yokohama Specie Bank) (Tokyo: Kyoikusha, 1980), 67, 237. According to Hijikata, the YSB's earliest overseas offices were located in New York (1880), London (1881), San Francisco (1886), Honolulu (1892), and Shanghai (1893). Ibid. 237–8. Tamaki Norio reports that, in addition, the YSB had established an agent's office in Lyons by 1889. See Tamaki Norio, 'The Yokohama Specie Bank: A Multinational in the Japanese Interest 1879–1931,' in Geoffrey Jones (ed.), *Banks as Multinationals* (London: Routledge, 1990), 196.

5. In March 1905, for example, the London branch of the YSB distributed prospectuses and application forms, and handled related business, for a 4.5 per cent sterling loan of £30 million for the Japanese imperial government. Yokohama shokin ginko (Yokohama Specie Bank), *Yokohama shokin ginko shi furoku* (Supplement to the history of the Yokohama Specie Bank) (Tokyo: Nihon keizai hyoronsha, 1976), iii. 719–24. The YSB arranged a number of other such loans in London at the time of the Russo–Japanese War. Comments of Ian Nish.

6. William D. Wray, *Mitsubishi and the N.Y.K., 1870–1914: Business Strategy in the Japanese Shipping Industry* (Cambridge, Mass.: Harvard University Press, 1984), 14, 248–9, 290, 308–11, 523–9.

7. Tokio Marine later (1899) closed this London office, and entrusted its local representation to Wills Trading Company. Nihon keieishi kenkyujo (Japan Business History Institute) (ed.), *Tokyo kaijo no 100 nen* (One hundred years of Tokio Marine) (Tokyo: Tokyo kaijo kasai hoken, 1979), 344–6.

8. Nihon keieishi kenkyujo (ed.), *Tokyo kaijo no 100 nen*, 79–86.

9. Wray, *Mitsubishi and the N.Y.K.*, 289, 308, 529.

10. See Hugh Patrick, 'Japan 1868–1914,' in Rondo Cameron (ed.), *Banking in the Early Stages of Industrialization* (New York: Oxford University Press, 1967), 267–8; and G. C. Allen, *A Short Economic History of Modern Japan* (London: 1962), 53, as cited in Mira Wilkins, 'Japanese Multinational Enterprise before 1914,' *Business History Review*, 60 (Summer 1986), 215 n.

11. Nihon keieishi kenkyujo (ed.), *Tokyo kaijo no 100 nen*, 345.

12. Mitsui & Co., *The 100-Year History of Mitsui & Co., Ltd.* (Tokyo: Mitsui & Co., 1977), 31–2.

13. Indeed, a Bank of Japan survey of Japanese business abroad reports that total foreign investments of Japanese companies stood at roughly $197 million in 1914. Of that amount, China accounted for roughly $152.7 million, followed by $24.6 million in the United States and Hawaii, and $19.7 million in the rest of the world. Apparently due to the small amounts involved, neither individual European countries nor even the European

region as a whole are mentioned by name in this official survey. Bank of Japan data, as reported in Wilkins, 'Japanese Multinational Enterprise before 1914,' 209.

14. Exceptions include the impacts of Japanese FDI on the pre-World War II French silk industry and on the turn-of-the-century London money markets. See below.

15. Mitsui & Co., *The 100-Year History of Mitsui & Co., Ltd.*, 81–2.

16. See, for example, Mira Wilkins, 'Japanese Multinationals in the United States: Continuity and Change, 1879–1990,' *Business History Review*, 64 (Winter 1990), 588–99; and Kawabe, 'Overseas Operations, 1868–1945,' 79–80.

17. Ando Yoshi, *Kindai nihon keizai shi yoran* (An overview of modern Japanese economic history) (Tokyo: Tokyo University Press, 1975), 23.

18. Yamazaki, 'General Trading Companies in Japan,' 34, 57; and Archives, PRO, BT 271/430. These firms, which included specialists in the textile trade together with generalists dealing in a wider range of commodities, all ranked among the top twenty Japanese trading companies in terms of paid-up capital during the mid-1920s. For a more detailed description of some of the chief activities of these companies, see Yamazaki, 'General Trading Companies in Japan,' 24–31.

19. Archives, PRO, BT 271/430.

20. Mishima Yasuo, 'Sekitan kaisha kara sogo shosha e: Mitsubishi Shoji' (From coal company to general trading company: Mitsubishi Corporation), in Miyamoto et al. (eds.), *Sogo shosha no keieishi*, 132; Hiroaki, 'General Trading Companies in Japan,' 33; Mitsubishi Shoji (Mitsubishi Corporation), *Mitsubishi Shoji: sono ayumi* (Mitsubishi Corporation: its development) (Tokyo: Mitsubishi Shoji, n.d.), 94; Kawabe Nobuo, 'Senzen ni okeru sōgō shosha no zaibei shiten katsudō: Mitsubishi Shōji San Furanshisuko, Shiattoru ryō shiten no jirei kenkyū' (The Pre-war Activities of the American Branches of the General Trading Companies: Case Studies of the Mitsubishi Corporation's Branch Offices in San Francisco and Seattle), *Keieishi gaku*, 16: 3 (Oct. 1981), 33; Nagasawa Yasuaki, 'The Overseas Branches of Mitsubishi Limited during the First World War: With Particular Reference to the London Branch,' *Japanese Yearbook on Business History*, 6 (1989), 132–3. Nagasawa reports that Mitsubishi Goshi (Mitsubishi Limited) established between 1915 and 1919 the trading operations throughout Europe later (1921) taken over by Mitsubishi Shoji (Mitsubishi Trading Company). Ibid., 133, 139.

According to French records, Mitsubishi's Paris office operated continuously until 1945. Archives Économiques et Financières, Ministère de l'Industrie, Cote 79, 0720/185, Compte rendu no. 204 of the Comité des Investissements Étrangers. In the inter-war period, Mitsubishi Shoji apparently became the dominant Japanese trading firm in Germany, whereas

Mitsui & Co. was key in the United Kingdom. Comments of Kudo Akira.

Kudo Akira also reports that Okura Shoji maintained an office in Germany as well during the years preceding World War II. See Kudo Akira, *Nichidoku kigyo kankeishi* (A history of Japanese–German industrial relations) (Tokyo: Yuhikaku, 1992), 30, 32.

21. See, for example, Kawabe, 'Overseas Operations, 1868–1945,' 84; Nagasawa, 'The Overseas Branches of Mitsubishi Limited during the First World War,' 126–8, 132.

22. Mitsui & Co., *The 100-Year History of Mitsui & Co., Ltd.*, 91. On Mitsubishi Shoji's third-country trade, see Nagasawa, 'The Overseas Branches of Mitsubishi Limited during the First World War,' 127–8, 132.

23. See, for example, Mitsui & Co., *The 100-Year History of Mitsui & Co., Ltd.*, 113; and Mark Mason, 'United States Direct Investment in Japan: Studies in Government Policy and Corporate Strategy' (Ph.D. dissertation, Harvard University, 1988), ch. 4.

24. Fujii Mitsuo et al. (eds.), *Nihon takokuseki kigyo no shiteki tenkai* (The Historical Development of Japanese Multinational Enterprises) (Tokyo: Otsuki Shoten, 1979), i. 153; Bank of England Archive OV 16/31. Mitsubishi Goshi operated a foreign exchange business out of its London office from 1916. This business was taken over by Mitsubishi Bank when the latter opened its London branch for business in 1920. Nagasawa, 'The Overseas Branches of Mitsubishi Limited during the First World War,' 123, 137–8.

25. Hijikata, *Yokohama shokin ginko*, 229. The YSB also operated an office in Lyons, but closed this office the same year it established the Paris and Berlin offices. Tamaki, 'The Yokohama Specie Bank,' 196–7, 212. In addition, the Bank of Chosen operated a London branch by 1931. Comments of Mira Wilkins.

26. On those services see, for example, Nakagawa Keiichiro, 'Ryotaisenkan no nihon kaiungyo' (The Japanese shipping industry in the inter-war period), in Nakagawa Keiichiro (ed.), *Ryotaisenkan no nihon kaiji sangyo* (The inter-war Japanese maritime industry) (Tokyo: Chuo daigaku shuppanbu, 1985), ch. 1. Also, see William Wray, 'NYK and the Commercial Diplomacy of the Far Eastern Freight Conference, 1896–1956,' in Yui Tsunehiko and Nakagawa Keiichiro (eds.), *Business History of Shipping: Strategy and Structure* (Tokyo: University of Tokyo Press, 1985), 279–305.

27. *Tokio kaijo no 100 nen*, 350–1; Archives, PRO, BT 271/488. The other Japanese insurance companies were Imperial, Kyodo, Nippon, Osaka, Tomei, and Yokohama.

28. For details, see Archives, PRO, BT 271/637.

29. See, for example, Yamazawa Ippei and Yamamoto Yuzo, *Boeki to kokusai shushi* (Foreign trade and balance of payments: estimates of long-term economic statistics of Japan since 1868) (Tokyo, 1979), as cited in Yasumuro

Kenichi, 'The Contribution of Sogo Shosha to the Multinationalization of Japanese Industrial Enterprises in Historical Perspective,' in Okochi Akio et al. (eds.), *Overseas Business Activities* (Tokyo: Tokyo University Press, 1984), 84; and Harold Moulton, *Japan: An Economic and Financial Appraisal* (Washington: Brookings Institution, 1931), 282–6. Indeed, in his extensive survey of foreign multinationals in British manufacturing and utilities before 1945, Geoffrey Jones listed a total of more than 120 such firms from 11 countries—but found that not even one came from Japan. See Geoffrey Jones, 'Foreign Multinationals and British Industry before 1945,' *Economic History*, 2nd Series, 41: 3 (1988), 429–53.

30. Kawabe, 'Overseas Operations, 1868–1945,' 92; *New York Times*, various issues.

31. Bank of England Archive OV16/117. Although located British records do not provide estimates of the total value of Japanese assets in the UK frozen by the British authorities in 1941, estimates of the value of all Japanese assets in the UK in 1952 (see below) and other related evidence suggest that the value of these frozen assets was not large.

32. Archives, PRO, BT 271/385, BT 271/637 and BT 271/654.

33. Article 1, Agreement between Japan and Germany Concerning Economic Cooperation, as cited in Mason, 'United States Direct Investment in Japan,' 232. According to an official analysis of the Allied Occupation of Japan's Supreme Commander for the Allied Powers, by this treaty '[b]oth governments [would] consider favorably applications for capital investments in industrial enterprises of the treaty partner's country.'

34. At least two factors help explain the apparent paucity of Japanese direct investment in wartime Germany. First, Japan took a far greater interest in investing in China, Manchuria, and elsewhere in Asia during the war years. And second, significant economic tensions between Germany and Japan also served to limit bilateral investment flows. (Similar to Japanese FDI trends in wartime Germany, German FDI apparently did not grow significantly in wartime Japan.) On (often cool) German–Japanese economic relations from the late 1930s, see, in particular, Kudo Akira, 'The Tripartite Pact and Synthetic Oil: The Ideal and Reality of Economic and Technical Cooperation between Japan and Germany,' *Occasional Papers in Social and Economic History*, Institute of Social Science, University of Tokyo, No. 4 (Mar. 1992) and Kudo, *Nichidoku kigyo kankeishi*; Mason, 'United States Direct Investment in Japan,' 232–3; and Erich Pauer, 'Lots of Friendship, but Few Orders: German–Japanese Economic Relations in the Late 1930s,' in Ian Nish (ed.), *German–Japanese Relations in the 1930's* (London: London School of Economics and Political Science, 1986), 10–37. Japan and Italy presumably entered into a similar cooperative economic arrangement in wartime, although the relative importance of such an accord surely would have been far less important than the German–Japanese tie.

35. Certain minor exceptions were permitted. See General Headquarters, Supreme Commander for the Allied Powers, 'Japanese Property Administration,' in 'History of the Nonmilitary Activities of the Occupation of Japan', ii: 'Reparations and Property Administration', Part C (unpublished), 65.
36. Ibid., 64ff. On the general results of this inventory, see 65–75.
37. Ibid., 74.
38. For the limited exceptions, see ibid., 74–5.
39. Archives, PRO, BT 271/385.
40. Ibid.
41. General Headquarters, Supreme Commander for the Allied Powers, 'Japanese Property Administration,' 75.
42. Ibid., 71. These estimates of external assets do not include Japanese military and naval *matériel* located abroad.
43. Archives, PRO, BT 271/429. By contrast, the British estimated that total Japanese assets in British territories in the Far East as of 1952 amounted to about £10 million. Ibid.
44. See, for example, Numaguchi Gen, 'Nihon no kaigai jigyo katsudo: sono rekishiteki katei to keieiteki shoyoin' (The Overseas Activities of Japanese Enterprise: The Historical Process and Various Managerial Factors), *Chiba Shodai ronso*, 13-B (June 1970), 252–7.
45. *Nihon Keizai Shimbun* (English edn.), Nov. 17, 1970.
46. According to one expert, during at least part of this era MITI required that prospective Japanese direct investors sign a written pledge that they would not export back to Japan goods which they might produce in overseas factories. See Michael Yoshino, 'The Multinational Spread of Japanese Manufacturing Investment since World War II,' *Business History Review*, 48 (Autumn 1974), 370–1.
47. On Japanese government policies and practices towards outward direct investment in this period, see Dennis Encarnation, *Rivals beyond Trade* (Ithaca, NY: Cornell University Press, 1992), 108; *Zaisei kinyu tokei geppo*, 452 (Dec. 1989), 3; Komiya Ryutaro, 'Japan's Foreign Direct Investment,' in Komiya Ryutaro, *The Japanese Economy: Trade, Industry and Government* (Tokyo: University of Tokyo Press, 1990), 117–18; and Hamada Koichi, 'Japanese Investment Abroad,' in Peter Drysdale (ed.), *Direct Foreign Investment in Asia and the Pacific* (Sydney: ANU, 1972), 188–9. Hamada suggests that concerns over loss of autonomous control over domestic monetary policy also may have figured among the government's motivations.
48. Encarnation, *Rivals beyond Trade*, 110; and Komiya, 'Japan's Foreign Direct Investment,' 118.
49. Archives Économiques et Financières, Ministère de l'Industrie, Cote 79, 0720/185, Compte rendu no. 204 of the Comité des Investissements Étrangers. It is possible that certain Japanese banks and insurance companies directly invested in post-war France prior to the entry of the

Mitsubishi Corporation, yet such investments apparently were not recorded in the Bank of Japan data as cited in Table 2.

50. Keizai hatten kyokai (Economic Development Association), *Fuyo Guruupu kigyo no kaigai jigyo* (The overseas enterprises of the Fuyo Group) (Tokyo: Keizai hatten kyokai, 1972), 112 ff.

51. Bank of England Archive, OV 16/83; Komiya, 'Japan's Foreign Direct Investment,' 248. These banks had been preceded by the Bank of Japan, however, which managed to open for business in London in late 1951. 'A very important position is occupied by England and other countries of the Sterling Area in Japan's progress toward realization of a self-supporting economy,' Bank of Japan Governor Ichimada Hisato had written to the British government in June 1951 explaining the reasons for his institution's interest in returning to London. 'It has been our earnest desire for some time to station a representative of this bank, a central bank, in London,' he went on, 'which is the nucleus of these areas and the economic and financial centre of Europe.' Bank of England Archive, OV 16/109.

52. Bank of England Archive, OV 16/83.

53. Akio Morita, *Made in Japan* (New York: Signet, 1988), 329. Also, see Table 2.

54. Ibid., 137–8. Also, see Table 2.

55. Ibid., 137–41, 324–30.

56. Kinugusa Yosuke, 'Japanese Firms' Foreign Direct Investment in the U.S.: The Case of Matsushita and Others,' in Okochi et al. (eds.), *Overseas Business Activities*, 30–1.

57. Toyota Motor Corporation, 'EC Market Unification and Toyota Activity in Europe,' unpublished report, 5.

58. Keizai hatten kyokai, *Fuyo Guruupu kigyo no kaigai jigyo*, 100–1; and Nissan Motor Co., Ltd., 'Facts File 1991' (unpublished report), 28–9.

59 Toyota Motor Company, 'EC Market Unification,' 5.

60. *Katagata Zenji Tatakau nihon kigyo* (Fighting Japanese enterprise) (Tokyo: Nihon keizai shinbunsha, 1967), 51 ff.; and Jiji shinsho (Jiji Press), *Nihon kigyo no kaigai shinshutsu: obei hen* (The overseas advance of Japanese enterprise: Europe and America) (Tokyo: Jiji Press, 1969), 172. Also, see Table 2.

61. MOF data, as cited in Yoshitomi Masaru et al., *Japanese Direct Investment in Europe: Motives, Impact and Policy Implications* (Aldershot: Avebury, 1991), 9.

62. For a description of the inward capital liberalization process, see Mark Mason, *American Multinationals and Japan: The Political Economy of Japanese Capital Controls, 1899–1980* (Cambridge, Mass.: Harvard University Press, 1992), ch. 5; and Dennis Encarnation and Mark Mason, 'Neither MITI nor America: The Political Economy of Capital Liberalization in Japan,' *International Organization*, 44: 1 (Winter 1990), 42–51.

63. Komiya, 'Japan's Foreign Direct Investment,' 118–20; Lawrence B. Krause and Sueo Sekiguchi, 'Japan and the World Economy,' in Hugh Patrick and

Henry Rosovsky (eds.), *Asia's New Giant: How the Japanese Economy Works* (Washington: Brookings Institution, 1976), 447.

64. Komiya, 'Japan's Foreign Direct Investment,' 120. Rising trade protectionism in the key American market and elsewhere also motivated Japanese business to invest abroad. See Encarnation, *Rivals beyond Trade*, 110.

65. Japan continued to invest large sums directly into Europe during the early 1990s, although neither during the 1990 nor 1991 Japanese fiscal years did annual outflows reach levels registered in the peak (fiscal) year of 1989.

66. F. N. Burton and F. H. Saelens, 'The European Investments of Japanese Financial Institutions,' *Columbia Journal of World Business* (Winter 1986), 32; and Fujii et al. (eds.), *Nihon takokuseki kigyo no shiteki tenkai*, ii. 92–3.

67. Fujii et al. (eds.), *Nihon takokuseki kigyo no shiteki tenkai*, ii. 94–5.

68. Ibid., 104–5.

69. Komiya, 'Japan's Foreign Direct Investment,' 126.

70. Burton and Saelens, 'The European Investments of Japanese Financial Institutions,' 30.

71. See, for example, Anthony Crowley, 'A Southern Spree,' *Far Eastern Economic Review* (Aug. 3, 1989), 55.

72. See, for example, Burton and Saelens, 'The European Investments of Japanese Financial Institutions,' 30–2; Jean-Michel Dinand, 'Séduire les banquiers japonais,' *France Japon Éco*, 45 (1991), 45–8; and Neil MacKinnon, 'Japanese Corporate and Financial Strategy in the Single European Market,' *European Management Journal*, 8: 3 (Sept. 1990), 313–20.

73. Fujii et al. (eds.), *Nihon takokuseki kigyo no shiteki tenkai*, ii. 40–1.

74. F. N. Burton and F. H. Saelens, 'Direct Investment by Sogo-Shosha in Europe,' *Journal of World Trade Law*, 17: 3 (May–June 1983), 249–58.

75. On the significance of the *sogo shosha* in bilateral trade between the EC and Japan during the 1980s see, for example, Stephen Thomsen and Phedon Nicolaides, *The Evolution of Japanese Direct Investment in Europe* (London: Harvester Wheatsheaf, 1991), 79–80.

76. Kinugusa, 'Japanese Firms' Foreign Direct Investment in the U.S.: The Case of Matsushita and Others,' 31; and Panasonic Europe (Headquarters) Ltd., 'Panasonic: Integrating with Europe,' company pamphlet, n.d., 18–20.

77. Toyota Motor Corporation, unpublished report, n.d.

78. Invest in Britain Bureau, 'List of Japanese Manufacturing Companies in the UK,' unpublished report, n.d.

79. DATAR, 'Liste des unités de production japonaises en France,' unpublished report, n.d.

80. Panasonic Europe (Headquarters) Ltd., 'Panasonic: Integrating with Europe,' 8–11, 18–20.

81. Toyota Motor Corporation, *Toyota: History of the First 50 Years* (Tokyo: Toyota Motor Corporation, n.d.), 494.

82. Fujii et al. (eds.), *Nihon takokuseki kigyo no shiteki tenkai*, ii. 166.

83. Japan Automobile Manufacturers Association, various pamphlets; company brochures.
84. MOF data, as cited in various MOF and BOJ publications, and in Yoshitomi et al., *Japanese Direct Investment in Europe*, 9.
85. The positions of these two regions as hosts to Japanese FDI inflows again reversed, however, in fiscal year 1994. Ministry of Finance.
86. Calculated on the basis of Japanese FDI data as reported by MOF through Mar. 1992.
87. Stefano Micossi and Gianfranco Viesti, 'Japanese Direct Manufacturing Investment in Europe,' in L. Alan Winters and Anthony J. Venables (eds.), *European Integration* (New York: Cambridge University Press, 1991), 207–8; Crowley, 'A Southern Spree,' 55. Indeed, Crowley echoed the author's own interview findings that, at least by 1989, there had developed a 'growing awareness' among Japanese managers and policymakers that a 'diffusion of Japanese investment throughout Europe, especially into the poorer southern states of the Continent' might well produce '*political* as well as economic rewards.' Emphasis added.
88. Ironically, however, if Europe follows the American example, total Japanese sales in Europe may substantially increase because of the potential import-stimulating effects of Japanese affiliates operating in the region. See Encarnation, *Rivals beyond Trade*, ch. 1.
89. See, for example, Fujii et al. (eds.), *Nihon takokuseki kigyo no shiteki tenkai*, ii. 2.
90. R. S. Sayers, *Bank of England Operations 1890–1914* (London: P. S. King & Son, Ltd., 1936), 40–2; Kanji Ishii, 'Japan,' in Rondo Cameron and V. I. Bovykin (eds.), *International Banking 1870–1914* (New York: Oxford University Press, 1991), 220–1. I am grateful to Geoffrey Jones for alerting me to the significant impacts of the YSB's London activities on the financial markets of the pre-1914 City of London.
    On the importance of the silk trade for Japan see, for example, Yokohama Shokin Ginko Chosabu (Research Section, Yokohama Specie Bank), *Kiito kinyu to gaikoku kawase* (Trade in raw silk thread and foreign exchange) (May 1926), 1–9.
    On some of the early effects of the silk trade on France as well as Japan, see, for example, Jean-Pierre Lehmann, 'The Silk Trade in the Bakumatsu Era and the Pattern of Japanese Economic Development,' in Ian Nish (ed.), *Bakumatsu and Meiji: Studies in Japan's Economic and Social History* (London: London School of Economics and Political Science, 1982), 39–55. According to Lehmann, Japan became a key source of raw silk and silkworm eggs for the Lyons-based silk industry as early as the mid-1860s. The silk industry, Lehmann reports, constituted a 'vital sector of the French economy' for many years thereafter—silken fabrics produced in Lyons alone, for example, accounted for no less than 7% of France's total exports in 1880—and Japan acted as a critical supplier to that industry.

91. On past European attitudes see, for example, R. P. T. Davenport-Hines and Geoffrey Jones, 'British Business in Japan since 1868,' in R. P. T. Davenport-Hines and Geoffrey Jones (eds.), *British Business in Asia since 1860* (New York: Cambridge University Press, 1989), 232; Ian Nish, 'Europe and Japan: A British Historian Looks at Misperceptions in the Inter-war Years,' a paper presented at the conference 'Europe and Japan: Cooperation and Conflict,' European Policy Unit, European University Institute, Florence, June 1992; and Endymion Wilkinson, *Japan versus the West: Image and Reality* (New York: Penguin Books, 1990), part III.

92. On more recent French reactions, see, for example, 'Japon: La Bataille d'Europe' (Japan: the battle of Europe), *Le Point*, 975 (May 27, 1991), 87–92; 'L'Invasion japonais' (The Japanese invasion), *Le Monde* (July 10, 1991), 1; and 'Édith peut-elle sauver nos industries: L'Obsession japonaise du premier ministre' (Can Edith save our industries: the Japanese obsession of the prime minister), *Le Nouvel Observateur* (May 23–9, 1991), 93. For an informative overview of more recent (but also historical) French perceptions of Japan and its economic position, see François Crouzet, 'Some French Views of Japan Today,' a paper presented at the conference 'Europe and Japan: Cooperation and Conflict,' European Policy Unit, European University Institute, Florence, June 1992.

93. Unless otherwise noted, the following discussion is based on Wilkins, 'Japanese Multinationals in the United States: Continuity and Change, 1879–1990,' 585–629.

94. Indeed, as in Europe, so, too, in America Japanese FDI historically was dominated by four types of firms: trading, finance, insurance, and shipping.

95. According to US Commerce Department data cited by Wilkins, for example, some 98% of all Japanese FDI in the United States in 1937 was in non-manufacturing sectors.

96. Indeed, according to Wilkins, by 1989 roughly one-quarter of all Japanese FDI in the United States was in manufacturing.

97. In 1989, for example, stocks of Japanese FDI in America represented roughly 17.4% of total FDI stocks in that country. US Department of Commerce *Survey of Current Business*, June 1990.

2

Automobiles

JAPANESE direct investment in the European automobile industry constituted one of the most important aspects of the larger economic challenge from Japan. Although Japanese auto firms had set up limited service and assembly operations in Europe during the post-war period, as noted above, not one such firm had ever manufactured automobiles in Europe before the 1980s. Particularly during the latter half of that decade, however, Nissan, Toyota, and many other Japanese car companies directly invested in major manufacturing operations within the European Community.[1]

The stakes for Europe were huge. In economic terms, for example, by 1990 the EC auto industry directly employed some 1.5 million and indirectly employed some 8.8 million European workers in manufacturing and related services, and accounted for roughly 9 per cent of industrial value added throughout the Community.[2] In addition, for Europeans in many countries the automotive industry constituted nothing less than a symbol of national industrial strength and technological prowess.[3] For these and other reasons, the sudden explosion of Japanese automobile investment in the EC provoked heated policy debates throughout the region.

The principal policy outcome which flowed from these debates was the creation in July 1991 of the EC–Japanese 'Elements of Consensus.' This landmark accord, together with related understandings between the Community and Japan, effectively placed numerical limits on Japanese motor vehicle exports to the EC as a whole and to specified member countries until the year 2000.[4] Moreover, complex and protracted negotiations also produced an arrangement which apparently placed implicit controls on Japan's European transplant factories.[5] Though highly controversial in part because the 'Elements' and related understandings were subject to widely varying interpretation, the accord nonetheless constituted Europe's principal policy response to the Japanese automobile challenge as unification approached.

To examine these and related issues, this chapter analyzes in particular the creation and significance of the 1991 EC–Japan motor vehicle accord.[6] First, salient features of Europe's automobile industry and the developing presence of Japanese cars in the region are examined. Second, the crafting of the 1991 arrangements and subsequent developments are explored. And finally, the chapter compares this European response with analogous American policy actions towards its own Japanese automotive challenge.

CONTEXT

The European Automobile Industry

Six firms or groups of firms accounted for the great majority of Western European car production as negotiations with Japan got underway.[7] These firms, in descending order of output, were: the Volkswagen Group (Audi, Seat, and VW), PSA (Peugeot, Citroën), the Fiat Group (Fiat, Lancia, Alfa, Innocenti, and Ferrari), the General Motors Group (GM/Opel, Saab), the Ford Group (Ford, Jaguar), and Renault. (See Table 5.) The size of these and other carmakers in Western Europe varied considerably, and included not only European-owned producers but also subsidiaries of American companies and, more recently, the local operations of Japanese auto firms as well. Despite the variety of companies and the diversity of their national origins, however, in their local markets domestically-owned firms generally outsold foreign-owned competitors by substantial margins. (See Table 6.)

By the late 1980s, many European-owned carmakers lagged considerably behind their foreign, and especially Japanese, counterparts. Studies conducted by MIT's International Motor Vehicle Program (IMVP), for example, suggested that the assembly plant productivity of European-owned volume producers in Europe substantially trailed productivity levels achieved by Japanese- (and often American-) owned assembly plants in Japan, North America, and even Europe.[8] In addition, studies by the IMVP and other groups suggested that, as compared with their Japanese counterparts in particular, Europe's volume manufacturers generally produced a smaller range of older and lower-quality automobiles, and failed to measure up to Japanese competition in other ways as well.[9]

Growing concerns over their international competitiveness led many European carmakers from the late 1980s to press for

TABLE 5. Western European car production, by company (1990)

Company	Number of units
Audi	421,378
Seat	323,900
Volkswagen	1,652,210
VW Group	2,397,488
Citroën	803,506
Peugeot	1,545,866
PSA	2,349,372
Alfa	223,643
Ferrari	4,292
Fiat	1,325,414
Innocenti	4,221
Lancia	313,166
Fiat Group	1,870,736
GM/Opel	1,663,562
Saab	87,356
GM Group	1,750,918
Ford	1,561,658
Jaguar	41,891
Ford Group	1,603,549
Renault	1,570,796
Mercedes	574,191
BMW	499,823
Rover	464,612
Volvo	369,840
Nissan	76,190
Porsche	32,162
Others	14,416
TOTAL	13,574,093

Source: Automotive Industry Data, Ltd., as cited in Automotive News, *Market Data Book 1992*, 2–3.

arrangements to secure public protection from greater Japanese competition through the 1990s. Most vocal in their calls for protection were, of course, those firms whose competitive positions were weakest and who therefore felt most vulnerable to the challenge from Japan. More than any other figure, PSA (hereafter, Peugeot)

TABLE 6. Percentage shares of EC automobile markets by company (1989)

Company	France	Germany	Italy	UK	Spain and Portugal	Rest of EC
VW Group	9.2	28.3	12.3	6.0	18.9	13.2
Fiat Group	7.3	4.8	57.2	3.4	9.0	6.2
PSA	32.8	3.6	7.7	8.9	17.4	13.1
Renault	29.0	3.4	7.1	3.8	19.3	7.1
Ford	7.1	10.1	4.8	26.4	13.1	10.1
GM	5.1	16.1	3.9	15.2	13.6	12.2
'Specialists'[a]	3.5	17.1	3.5	8.2	4.4	8.0
Japanese	2.8	15.1	1.4	11.1	1.8	24.8
Rover	1.7	0.2	0.9	13.6	1.3	1.0
Others	1.4	1.1	1.0	3.2	0.8	4.3
TOTAL	100.0	100.0	100.0	100.0	100.0	100.0

[a] 'Specialists' refers to the (principally German) luxury carmakers.

Source: Automobile Industry Data, Ltd., *Market Data Book* (1990), as adapted by Steven Tolliday in 'Globalization or Regionalization: The European Automobile Industry Faces 1992,' Harvard Business School Case No. 9-391-207.

Chairman Jacques Calvet—the Lee Iacocca of the European automobile industry—openly and vigorously lobbied for such protection.[10] Pointing to the potentially severe consequences of increased Japanese market penetration for Europe's large auto companies—and convinced that European carmakers faced enormous obstacles to entry into the Japanese market—Calvet called for strict limits on Japanese auto firms' participation in the European Community after the projected completion of the internal market at the end of 1992. Joining Calvet in calling for substantial protection against the Japanese from the late 1980s were, among others, Fiat Chairman Giovanni Agnelli and Renault CEO Raymond Levy.[11]

Not all carmakers in Europe lobbied for protection from Japanese competition during the late 1980s, however. Perhaps most notably, the German luxury car specialists Mercedes, BMW, and Porsche believed they could effectively compete against Japanese makers even in a unified EC market, and worried about the implications of protectionist moves in Europe for their own vehicle sales in Japan and, especially, America. In addition, they were joined by fellow German producer VW, whose Chairman Carl Hahn hesitated at this point to seek protection from Japanese competitors. Hahn understood that Japan's producers represented a major challenge to VW, but opposed restrictions in part because he believed that the rigors of the open market ultimately would strengthen VW and the rest of the European auto industry. And finally, the British Rover Group previously had entered into a strategic alliance with Honda, and later sold 20 per cent of its equity to that Japanese producer.[12] With this relationship in place, Rover declined to join those pressing for protection. During the course of the negotiations, however, the perceptions (and positions) of some of these European firms would change substantially.

Japanese Strategies, European Policies

Japanese automobile exports to Europe generally remained insignificant through the 1960s. Within the European Community, Japanese market share (supplied almost entirely through exports) by 1970 had exceeded a mere 1 per cent only in a few smaller EC markets such as those of Portugal, Belgium, Denmark, and the Netherlands. In the larger auto markets of the EC, by contrast, Japanese market share data suggest that by that same year exports from Japan were extremely small. Japanese auto firms in 1970 together held just 0.4 per cent of the British market, for example, 0.2 per cent of the French market, and negligible shares of the German and Italian markets.[13]

During the 1970s, however, Japan's exports and market shares rose considerably in virtually all the markets of the Community. Indeed, by 1980 Japanese auto firms had attained enormous shares in EC markets such as Belgium (24.7 per cent), the Netherlands (26.4 per cent), Denmark (30.9 per cent), Ireland (30.8 per cent), and Greece (42.9 per cent). In addition, by that year Japan's carmakers had attained sizable shares of the British (11.9 per cent), French (2.9 per cent), and German (10.4 per cent) markets (although long-standing restrictions, described below, had kept Japan's share in Italy to just 0.14 per cent).[14] From a minor position in 1970, Japanese auto companies together had thus managed to attain, almost entirely through exports, major positions in most of the Community's automobile markets just ten years later.

Rising Japanese exports to Europe encouraged many host governments to implement (or extend) policies designed to limit the numbers of imported Japanese cars.[15] In 1975, for example, Britain obliged Japan to limit Japanese auto imports to 11 per cent of the UK automobile market. Two years later, the French government effectively placed a ceiling on Japanese car imports of just 3 per cent.[16] Spain and Portugal later restricted Japanese market shares to 1 per cent and 14 per cent, respectively. And an official bilateral accord dating from 1954 effectively enabled the Italian government to continue limiting Japanese imports to small (always less than 2 per cent) shares of Italy's automobile market in subsequent years.[17] These five EC nations—together with West Germany, which in 1981 had forged an informal agreement to limit Japanese auto imports to no more than roughly 15 per cent of the local market—would continue to impose quantitative restrictions on Japanese auto imports throughout the 1980s.[18] In addition, Japan's penetration of numerous European markets was further limited by member state-sanctioned exclusive dealership systems.[19]

Japanese firms continued to ship substantial numbers of automobiles to Europe in the 1980s, but the imposition of European restrictions effectively braked or sharply restrained Japanese market share growth in many Community markets during this decade. Although Japan's market share in Germany increased from 10.4 per cent to 15.2 per cent and in Italy increased from 0.14 per cent to 1.41 per cent during the years 1980 to 1989, for example, it actually *declined* in Britain from 11.9 per cent to 11.3 per cent and in France from 2.9 per cent to 2.8 per cent in this same period. Despite these restrictions, however, Japanese automobile firms together maintained important shares of the total European market at the end of the 1980s. (See Table 7.) Indeed, in 1989 Japan held roughly one-tenth of the overall EC market, supplied almost entirely by exports, which numbered some 1.23 million vehicles.[20]

The post-war development of Japan's motor vehicle exports to the Community encouraged Japanese foreign direct investment in the EC first to support and, later, to complement this trade. Japanese carmakers, as noted above, began to invest directly in the region from the 1960s. Toyota and Nissan, for example, both established marketing operations in Europe during this period. Moreover, by the late 1970s, virtually all of Japan's major auto manufacturers had directly invested in European assembly plants.

The threat of increased EC protectionism and other factors motivated Japanese automakers to expand their direct investments into

TABLE 7. Japanese shares of European automobile markets, by company (1989)

Company	Market share (%)
Nissan	2.9
Toyota	2.5
Mazda	1.8
Mitsubishi	1.2
Honda	1.0
Suzuki	0.6
Subaru	0.4
Daihatsu	0.3
Isuzu	0.1
TOTAL	10.8

Source: Automobile Industry Data, Ltd., *Market Data Book* (1990), as adapted by Steven Tolliday in 'Globalization or Regionalization: The European Automobile Industry Faces 1992,' Harvard Business School Case No. 9-391-207.

local manufacturing in the Community starting in the 1980s. Although some EC member states remained leery of the prospects of major Japanese auto plants operating within their borders, the advent of the Thatcher government led the British authorities aggressively to encourage Japanese FDI in the United Kingdom.[21] Attractive incentives packages were the centerpiece of the British policy to attract Japanese auto firms, but together with these incentives Japan's car companies had 'voluntarily' to accept performance requirements in the form of specified minimum (generally starting at 60 per cent but later rising to 80 per cent) local (EC, not UK) content levels. (See Appendix I.)

Nissan was the first Japanese firm to respond to Britain's overtures when, in 1984, Japan's second largest automaker concluded an agreement with the British government to establish a major production facility in England.[22] Honda followed Nissan's lead by launching its own project to set up a British plant (with Rover) in 1985, followed by an Isuzu initiative (with GM) and a Toyota direct investment in the UK in 1987 and 1989, respectively.[23] This British FDI policy, as we shall see, would carry important implications for

Community negotiations with the Japanese in the early 1990s over future automobile trade and investment restrictions. Nissan also directly invested in Spain (with local capital) and Toyota in Germany (with VW) during the 1980s, but well before the end of the decade it had become clear that Japan's major automakers had chosen the UK as the principal site of their European manufacturing activities. (See Table 8.)

Approval of the EC's Single European Act (SEA) in 1986 thrust new challenges before member states determined to continue protecting their domestic automobile companies from Japanese competition. Under the terms of the Act, all EC member states were obliged to remove restrictions on the movement of goods within the Community by the end of 1992.[24] Since numerous EC governments did not impose quotas on auto imports from Japan, this obligation would enable Japanese firms to export vehicles to erstwhile protected EC countries via non-restricted Community markets. In addition, of course, completion of the internal market raised the possibility that Japanese transplant factories would produce autos in one EC country (the United Kingdom, for example) and then freely ship them to other EC countries (France and Italy, for instance).[25] The approaching changes in Community policy together with the lagging competitive positions of many European automakers therefore placed increasing pressure on certain EC states to find new ways to support their domestic auto firms.[26]

ACCORD

Process

The Japanese automobile challenge to the unifying European Community led to long, complex, and often bitter negotiations involving numerous players from the EC and Japan. MITI officials represented the Japanese side in bilateral talks, though among government agencies the Ministry of Foreign Affairs also sought to influence the process. In addition, Japan's major carmakers consulted with government negotiators both individually and through the Japanese Automobile Manufacturers' Association (JAMA), the industry group then under the rotating presidency of Nissan's outspoken President Yutaka Kume. Recommended tactics and issue emphases occasionally differed among these players, yet on the

TABLE 8. Japanese manufacturing FDI in the EC motor vehicle industry (1992)

Country	Company name	Equity shares	Start-up date	Annual production capacity
United Kingdom				
Nissan	Nissan Motor M'fing (UK)	Nissan: 100%	July 1986	300,000 units
Honda	Honda of the UK M'fing	Honda: 80%	October 1989	100,000 cars
		Rover: 20%		70,000 engines
Isuzu	IBC Vehicles	GM: 60%	September 1989	60,000–70,000 units
		Isuzu: 40%		
Toyota	Toyota Motor M'fing (UK)	Toyota: 100%	Mid-1992	200,000 engines
	Toyota Motor M'fing (UK)	Toyota: 100%	Late 1992	200,000 cars
Germany				
Toyota	Volkswagen	—	January 1989	15,000 units
Spain				
Nissan	Nissan Motor Iberica	Nissan: 67.6%	January 1983	80,000 units
		Local: 32.4%		
Portugal				
Toyota	Salvador Caetano, IMVP	Toyota: 27%	October 1968	12,000 units
		Local: 73%		

Source: Adapted from JAMA, *The Motor Industry of Japan: 1992* (JAMA: Tokyo, 1992).

whole they had established a general consensus on the major questions in the talks.

If the Japanese actors were relatively few and in general agreement on the central issues, however, the European side represented diverse players with varying interests. Bilateral negotiations on the European side were led by the Commission's Directorate-General for External Relations (DG I), yet the Internal Market and Industry (DG III) and, to a lesser extent, the Competition (DG IV) Directorates-General also played important roles in the bargaining process. Behind Commission negotiators, moreover, stood officials from the twelve Community governments. These governments each sent representatives to the Council of Ministers, the Community body which held formal power over the actions of the Commission. And finally, some of the major European carmakers also figured prominently in the bargaining process. These various Community players at times stood in general agreement, but more often pursued differing (and, at times, shifting) interests and goals.[27]

The process which culminated in the EC–Japan auto accord took more than three years to complete, and passed through four more or less distinct phases.[28] The first and longest phase ran from early 1988 through the end of 1989, and chiefly involved representatives of the European Commission together with officials from EC member states. The initiative to revise Community policy towards Japanese automobiles came principally from the Commission. Aware that completion of the internal market would require major changes in the auto policies of numerous member states, in early 1988 DG III began to study the position and likely development of the region's car industry. This work led to completion of an internal report entitled 'The Future of the EC Auto Industry,' circulated within the Commission in September 1989. DG III then combined this and other internal reports with externally commissioned research to provide a basis for future policy discussions.

Despite the central role of the Commission in initiating this first stage of the process, however, the critical direct and indirect roles of member states soon became apparent. With research in hand, Commissioner Martin Bangemann and DG III officials embarked upon an intensive consultation process with individual member states.[29] The positions of these states initially divided into four principal groups. Least influential in (and least directly affected by) this process were the six states without significant domestic auto industries:

Automobiles

Belgium, Denmark, Greece, Ireland, Luxembourg, and the Netherlands.[30] These states naturally stood to gain little, if anything, by limiting Japanese cars in the EC after 1992, but chose to remain largely silent throughout the long process. This they did largely to appease their more concerned (and generally more powerful) fellow Community members, and to earn political capital useful in future EC bargaining. The United Kingdom staked out a second position. Although it was no longer home to a major auto industry controlled by domestic interests, the UK hosted not only the local subsidiaries of the American firms Ford and General Motors, but also the newly arrived and growing Japanese operations of Nissan, Honda, and Toyota. In their talks with the Commission, UK representatives favored complete freedom for Japanese transplants to produce and ship their goods throughout the Community, but quietly signalled their willingness to support continued controls over Japanese auto imports.

Two other groups of member states maintained still different views. The 'Latin 4' of France, Italy, Spain, and Portugal were home to the domestic auto companies which felt most threatened by Japanese competition. Led by the French government, this 'Club Med' of the Community pressed for strong controls over Japanese participation in the EC auto industry after 1992. The (West) German government represented a fourth position during this early stage of the process. Though concerned about the future role of Japan in Community auto markets, German officials initially opposed controls on Japanese cars in part because, as previously suggested, many of their own automakers remained confident and feared retaliation.

Following talks with member states, in mid-1989 the Commission began a process of inter-service consultations which finally produced an official EC position on the Japanese automobile question. Representatives of DG I, III, and IV all took part in the consultations. Moreover, the Commission in July 1989 formed a special *ad hoc* committee on automobiles composed of seven Cabinet members to facilitate and coordinate internal discussions. These various Commission players worked through that autumn to define a common position which generally met the requirements of the SEA as well as the special interests of vitally affected member states. Finally, in December 1989, the Commission settled on a list of broad principles designed to meet most of these various (though partially conflicting) demands. These principles reflected, among other things, the determination to limit Japanese auto exports to the Community during a finite period of time and to seek Community assistance for domestic automakers to help in their restructuring process. Less clear, however, was policy towards Japan's local transplants.

The process entered a second critical stage in January 1990, when representatives of the European Commission and MITI began officially to consider how to modify and implement the general principles worked out the previous month. Following the issuance by the Council of Ministers of what amounted to an unofficial 'oral mandate'—remaining differences between member states, worries that an official (and therefore publicly announced) position would weaken the EC's bargaining position, and fears that any official agreement limiting Japanese autos in the Community resulting from these talks might violate GATT rules discouraged the issuance of a formal, written Council mandate to negotiate—the Commission contacted MITI to hammer out a draft bilateral accord. This round of talks dealt not only with Japanese auto imports into the Community as a whole, but also with imports into certain specific EC markets as well as the highly sensitive issue of Japanese transplant production and other matters.[31] MITI negotiators indicated flexibility in entertaining a number of possible restrictions in the proposed EC–Japan accord, but insisted in particular that no transplant restrictions of any kind be incorporated in such an agreement. On the basis of these discussions, Commission and MITI negotiators settled on a draft accord in August 1990 dubbed (by a DG I official) the 'Elements of Consensus'.

The draft 'Elements' set forth a number of more or less defined positions. For example, the Commission and MITI agreed on a transition period of between five and seven years from the projected completion of the internal market in January 1993 during which time Japanese auto imports would be restricted. This draft document also specified overall limits on cars which could be imported into the Community as a whole from Japan by the end of the transition period, although no estimates were offered for interim years and actual numbers would depend on the development of the local market. On the basis of these figures, the Commission anticipated that, including transplant production within the Community, Japan would be able to increase its share of the total EC car market from roughly 10 per cent in 1989 to about 21 per cent between 1997 and 1999. The draft also set fixed future ceilings on Japanese imports into the five countries with explicit Japanese quota arrangements, a 'no targeting' clause to prevent concentrated Japanese transplant sales in countries with such quantitative restrictions, and a semi-annual monitoring mechanism to ensure that the terms of the accord were faithfully executed.

Community states and carmakers then deliberated the merits of the proposed 'Elements' during a critical third phase of the process which lasted from roughly September 1990 through early April 1991. Shortly after the Commission and MITI had completed their draft 'Elements,' DG III Commissioner Martin Bangemann set off a lively and protracted debate within the European automobile industry when he convened a meeting of the heads of three of the four EC mass auto producers (Fiat, Renault, and VW, but not Peugeot) to try to 'sell' them the proposed accord.[32] Bangemann understood that the EC's major volume carmakers felt most vulnerable to increased Japanese competition in the Community, and that their reactions to the draft 'Elements' would critically affect the positions of their governments and, therefore, the ultimate success of the proposed accord.

Much to Bangemann's (and the Commission's) dismay, however, these three European volume carmakers (together with the fourth, Peugeot, after it had learned of the discussions) rejected the draft 'Elements' as too favorable towards Japan, and resolved instead to forge a common industry position which met their requirements. Having reviewed voluminous and mounting evidence pointing to their acute vulnerability to Japanese competition, these carmakers had concluded that they would need far more protection than outlined in the draft 'Elements' successfully to meet the competition from Japan. Significantly, Fiat, Peugeot, and Renault were here joined by erstwhile free trader Carl Hahn, the chairman of VW, who would soon proclaim publicly what he had already concluded privately—that 'All Europeans are now vulnerable' to unfettered Japanese automobile competition in the Community.[33]

On October 1, 1990, the heads of the four mass producers—Agnelli (Fiat), Calvet (Peugeot), Levy (Renault), and Hahn (VW)—met to forge a common position which they intended to communicate to the Commission. Agnelli, Levy, and Hahn first drafted a letter setting out their joint position, which called for a longer transition period—up to ten years in length—before Japanese auto exports could gain unrestrained access to the Community, together with limits on Japanese transplant production during this period. Peugeot's Calvet, however, refused to sign the common letter when presented with it. Instead, he called for even tougher measures against the Japanese, including in particular a halt to the development of Japanese transplant projects throughout the Community. Unable to convince Calvet to back down from his demands, the three authors of the joint position abandoned their idea to send the draft letter to the Commission. The meeting then broke up.

Unsuccessful in their efforts to forge a common position in this October meeting, the Fiat, Renault, and VW chiefs chose to craft a common stance through a reconstituted European automobile industry association. These three understood that the original association, the Comité des Constructeurs du Marché Commun (Committee of Common Market Manufacturers, or CCMC), made all decisions by unanimous vote—which meant that Calvet could derail any future efforts to create a position acceptable to all (fourteen) CCMC members. In February 1991 they therefore created a new organization—the Association des Constructeurs Européens d'Automobiles (Association of European Automobile Manufacturers, or ACEA)—and wrote into the new organization's by-laws a provision which enabled members to make decisions by majority rather than unanimous vote.[34] Calvet was then invited to join this new association, but declined the offer when he realized that, alone, he could no longer block the will of the other industry members.

In its reconstituted form, the association quickly managed to agree on a common position with specific recommendations for an accord with the Japanese. This position, like the industry document prepared the previous October, advocated a transition period longer than that contained in the 'Elements' together with clear limits on Japanese transplant production. In addition, the ACEA called for a division of market growth between Japanese and European producers, a decrease in Japanese volume if the market contracted, and a Japanese market share cap of roughly 15 per cent—including transplant production—by the end of the transition period. Following completion and approval of this platform by member companies in March 1991, ACEA member firms were assigned the task of convincing their respective home governments to support the common industry stance. In addition, the Association sent a four-page memorandum to the Commission setting forth its position.

Based in part on the reactions of their domestic carmakers, key EC member governments refined their own positions and instructed the Commission to modify its negotiating stance accordingly. Perhaps most importantly, the 'Latin 4' had by now solidified their views and constituted what one Commission official termed a 'blocking coalition' at the Community level to prevent any accord which they deemed too 'soft' on the Japanese. Specifically, these member states, largely following the wishes of their domestic auto firms, demanded among other things a minimum seven-year transition period from January 1, 1993, together with added clauses in the draft specifying changes in Japanese import levels if development of the Community market exceeded or fell short of anticipated levels during the life of the accord. They also pressed for some means explicitly to include Japanese transplant production in any final accord. Yet the 'Latin 4' chose not to press for a ten-year transition period and other maximum demands expressed by their domestic firms, for these states generally believed that vigorous Japanese competition would speed desirable restructuring by their firms.

Greatly influenced by increasing concerns over Japanese competition even among its former free trader specialist carmakers, the German government in a critical development quietly tilted in favor of most of the demands set forth by the common Latin front. The Germans apparently refused, however, to back explicit limits on the Japanese transplants. The British government, for its part, publicly stressed strong opposition to any controls over Japanese transplants in the Community, but again expressed privately its willingness to support restrictions on Japanese auto imports. Based essentially on the positions of these six key governments, Commission representatives by the end of April had adopted a tougher position which they then presented to their MITI counterparts.[35]

MITI, however, refused to accept all of the new EC proposals—which led to a fourth, and final, phase requiring some three months of negotiation from April 1991. Although MITI representatives now professed a willingness to accept among other EC proposals a full seven-year transition period, together with the British they remained firmly opposed in particular to any clause formally limiting the number of cars which could be produced by the Japanese transplants. Japanese officials apparently were concerned, above all, that any such clause might create a precedent which would tempt the United States to imitate European practice.

This impasse was broken only by the Cabinet of EC Commission President Jacques Delors, which proposed that the Commission merely issue a unilateral oral declaration at the conclusion of the talks suggesting a link between the levels of transplant production and Japanese imports to the Community. In exchange, the Commission agreed to drop a number of other outstanding issues.[36] Before finalizing these arrangements, however, the Commission had to convince the French, in particular, to drop their concerns that the accord still was not tough enough on the Japanese. To persuade the French to go along, the Commission discreetly held out the carrot of significant future Community assistance for the restructuring of France's auto industry, and the stick of tougher enforcement of EC competition rules against French quotas on Japanese imports by local car distributors. French European Affairs Minister Élizabeth Guigou, charged with representing her government at the Council of Ministers, found herself caught between the liberal-leaning Minister of Industry Roger Farroux and the hardline inclinations of Prime Minister Édith Cresson.[37] Minister Guigou appealed directly to President François Mitterrand, who apparently judged that the imperative of Community consensus together with the promises and implied threats of the Commission outweighed any remaining concerns about the accord. These last disagreements resolved, the European Commission and MITI struck a final deal.

Outcome

The negotiations between Japan and the Community produced one of the most unusual understandings in modern international economic diplomacy. At the heart of these understandings, announced on July 31, 1991, was a substantially revised 'Elements of Consensus,' a bilateral document which set forth a series of goals and measures concerning Japanese motor vehicles in the EC through the end of the decade. The Commission and the Japanese government adopted three common goals: first, the 'progressive' and, ultimately, 'full liberalization' of the EC motor vehicle market; second, 'avoidance' of EC market 'disruption' by Japanese vehicle exports; and third, a (Japanese) 'contribution]' to enable EC manufacturers to attain 'adequate levels' of 'international competitiveness' by the granting of a 'transitional period' during which Community markets would remain regulated.

To attain these various goals, the parties agreed on a series of measures pertaining to Japanese participation in the EC motor vehicle market through December 31, 1999. First, the Commission promised that Community members would immediately begin to ease relevant national restrictions and measures taken under Article 115 of the Treaty of Rome, and would abolish such restrictions and measures no later than January 1, 1993.

Second, the two sides agreed that Japan would 'monitor' through semi-annual consultations vehicle exports to the EC as a whole and to each 'restricted' EC market—what Bangemann called the 'double lock' on Japanese auto shipments to the Community—during a transition period to end on December 31, 1999. Specific export levels were provisionally set for the 1999 calendar year. These levels, however, were based on market forecasts, and both sides agreed that changes in actual market conditions would require revisions in Japanese export limits. The 1999 'forecast level' of Japanese vehicle exports to the EC as a whole was set at 1.23 million vehicles— virtually the same level as the 1989 figure—or roughly 8.1 per cent of the estimated EC market of 15.1 million vehicles in 1999. In addition, the 'Elements' set forth 'forecast levels' of Japanese vehicle exports to each of the five 'restricted' EC markets. Based on total anticipated demand in each of these markets, these 'forecast levels' indicated that Japanese producers would capture through imports roughly 5.3 per cent of the French, Italian, and Spanish markets, 7.0 per cent of the UK market, and 8.4 per cent of the Portuguese market in 1999. (See Table 9.)

Third, the 'Elements' addressed the issue of the Japanese transplants in the Community. In one part of the document, the Commission pledged that the EC would impose neither 'restrictions on Japanese investment' nor controls on 'the free circulation of its products in the Community.' At the same time, however, the Japanese side agreed to 'convey' to Japanese vehicle makers the Commission's 'repeatedly expressed concern' that concentrated sales in specified national markets of motor vehicles *produced by these makers in the Community* would create serious 'market disruption' and significantly frustrate the efforts of EC makers to attain international levels of competitiveness.

TABLE 9. Japanese automobile exports to select EC countries in 1999: levels as agreed in the 'Elements of Consensus'

Country	Anticipated total EC market demand (units)	Anticipated Japanese market share through imports (units)	Anticipated Japanese market share through imports (%)
France	2,850,000	150,000	5.3
Italy	2,600,000	138,000	5.3
Spain	1,475,000	79,000	5.3
United Kingdom	2,700,000	190,000	7.0
Portugal	275,000	23,000	8.4

Source: 'Elements of Consensus'.

In addition to the 'Elements of Consensus,' the EC and Japan simultaneously circulated to certain interested parties a number of unilateral interpretations and clarifications which touched on various points contained in the bilateral agreement. EC Vice President Frans Andriessen (in Brussels) and MITI Vice Minister Eiichi Nakao (in Tokyo), the nominal heads of the two negotiating teams, appended to the 'Elements,' for example, individual statements largely reiterating various points already contained in them. Further, the EC side issued an 'Internal Declaration' which specified the Commission's interpretation of two items set forth in the accord: first, the Commission held that Community manufacturers should enjoy at least one-third of any EC market growth beyond estimated levels throughout the transitional period; and second, the Commission expected that Japanese manufacturers would reduce their exports by 75 per cent of the proportionate drop in any overall EC market decline.

Finally, and most significantly, issued together with the 'Elements' were written versions of a carefully scripted and coordinated 'conclusive' oral declaration made by Andriessen to Nakao, together with Nakao's oral response to Andriessen. Andriessen stated in his declaration that, in its negotiations with Japan, the Commission adopted the 'working assumption' that 'Japanese owned factories located in the EC' would produce for sale in the Community roughly 1.2 million motor vehicles by the end of the

TABLE 10. Japanese automobile market shares in select EC countries in 1999: Commission estimates based on internal working assumptions

Country	Anticipated Japanese market share through imports (%)	Anticipated Japanese market share through transplants (%)	Total anticipated Japanese market share (%)
France	5.3	1.7–5.7	7–11
Italy	5.3	1.7–5.7	7–11
Spain	5.3	6.8–10.8	12.1–16.1
United Kingdom	7.0	13.9–19.9	20.9–26.9
Portugal	8.4	8.1–13.1	16.5–21.5

Source: Internal Commission documents.

transition period. Significantly, Nakao did not directly challenge this assumption, but rather 'called' Andriessen's 'attention' to the Commission's promise in the 'Elements' not to restrict 'Japanese investment or sales of its products' in the Community. The Commission's working assumption on total Japanese transplant sales in the Community, together with estimates of total Japanese exports to the region contained in the 'Elements,' suggested that Japan would capture roughly 16.1 per cent of the total EC automobile market by 1999. In addition, internal EC estimates of transplant sales in each of the five restricted markets, together with projected Japanese exports to each of these markets as set forth in the 'Elements,' also enabled the Commission to generate estimates of total Japanese market shares in these five countries for 1999. (See Table 10.)

Denouements

Conclusion of this historic accord did not, of course, put an end to disputes over Japanese motor vehicle penetration of Community markets. To the contrary, conflicting interpretations of that accord provoked new disagreements beginning virtually the day of its announcement. These disagreements at times pitted Japan against the Community as a whole, but at other times caused deep divisions within the EC itself.

The proper interpretation of the accord's limits on Japanese exports produced a number of controversies between Japan and the

Community. Beginning in the fall of 1992 and lasting more than six months thereafter, for example, the two sides disagreed over prospects for total 1993 EC new car demand—and, therefore, over allowable limits on Japanese auto imports during the first year of the accord's operation. On April 1, 1993, MITI and the Commission finally reached an accord based on a bilateral consensus of estimated 1993 Community demand, yet significant disagreements arose in subsequent consultations as well.[38] In addition, the Community and Japan continued to ponder the implications of the accord for exports to the EC of Japanese-badged motor vehicles produced in third countries—what the French sometimes call 'diverted exports.' Though such exports are nowhere mentioned in the 'Elements' or related statements, Japanese pursuit of this third-country strategy could still provoke relevant debates left unsettled in the 1991 arrangements.[39] Indeed, Honda did soon export some of its Accord models from its Ohio plant to the EC.[40] In addition, Mitsubishi Motors—the only major Japanese motor vehicle manufacturer without a transplant factory in the EC—started to export to the EC its automobiles and pickup trucks produced in Australia, Malaysia, and Turkey.[41]

The issue of controls over Japanese transplant production in the Community provoked at least equally great controversy, although here the arguments caused division within the EC as well as between the Community and Japan. On one side stood some of the Latin hardliners, who insisted that the accord placed a strict upper limit of 1.2 million vehicles produced at Japanese transplants through the 1990s. Not surprisingly, Peugeot's Calvet was among the most vociferous proponents of this view.[42] Somewhat more surprisingly, however, even such widely quoted Japanese sources as *Nihon keizai shimbun (Nikkei)*—the closest Japanese equivalent of the *Financial Times* or the *Wall Street Journal*—also suggested that Japan in fact agreed to observe limits on transplant production by failing directly to contradict Andriessen's oral declaration in the carefully prepared exchange with Nakao. 'It will be difficult to expand local production beyond the number . . . forecast by the EC, since Japan did not forthrightly oppose it,' *Nikkei*, for example, stated in its lead editorial shortly after announcement of the accord.[43] Indeed, Japan's 'implicit acceptance' of the transplant number, *Nikkei* went on, 'set the limit for the expansion of transplant production.'[44]

Opposed to this viewpoint were the British and Japanese

governments in particular, who maintained that the accord in no way restricted either the operation of Japanese motor vehicle factories in the Community or the movement of products made at these plants within the EC. 'I am pleased,' stressed, for example, the then UK Trade and Industry Secretary Peter Lilley at the announcement of the accord, 'that the Community has accepted there shall be no restriction on Japanese motor car manufacturing investment in the EC or on the freedom to sell the vehicles produced throughout the EC.'[45] MITI officials publicly offered similar views, as did JAMA Chairman and Nissan President Kume, who stated unequivocally: 'Whether [Japanese transplant production in the EC during the life of the accord] will be 1.2 million or not, this is what the EC Commission said unilaterally. This is not something that will bind the Japanese side.'[46]

Although these two viewpoints stand in contradiction, the text of the accord together with commentary by those who drafted it and other considerations suggest that the EC–Japan arrangement did indeed place implicit (though somewhat vague and ambiguous) limits on the Japanese transplants. First, the 'Elements' themselves include language warning Japanese carmakers against concentrating sales from their European transplant factories in the five restricted markets during the life of the agreement. Second, the fact that the chief Commission negotiator, following intensive consultations with the French and other member governments, clearly articulated to his MITI counterpart—and was not directly challenged by this counterpart—that the Community assumed Japanese transplant factories would produce for sale in the EC 1.2 million units by 1999, certainly suggests the possibility of an informal arrangement limiting Japanese firms to that level during the life of the accord. And third, interviews with Commission representatives and others suggest that, in interpreting the accord and related arrangements, the Commission might well compensate for any Japanese transplant production above negotiated levels by adjusting downward permissible levels of Japanese auto imports into the Community.[47] Therefore, although some of the precise implications of the accord for the operation of Japan's Community transplants remain controversial, through the 1991 bilateral understanding the European Community apparently managed to institute implicit controls on Japanese foreign direct investment in the EC automobile industry. Yet the (surely deliberate) ambiguities of interpreting and implementing measures relating to these transplants virtually assure that this issue will remain a point of great contention for years to come.

These and other ongoing disputes surrounding the 1991 accord point to continued conflict over Japanese penetration of the European Community's automobile markets. 'The agreement is politically fragile both within the EC and between the EC and Japan,' one observer rightly noted. 'There are big questions that won't go away.'[48] Indeed, official EC and Japanese statements notwithstanding, many experts believe that the Community will erect still new protections from Japanese competition even after the termination of the accord.[49]

EUROPE, AMERICA, AND THE JAPANESE AUTOMOTIVE CHALLENGE

As the Single Market approached, Europe crafted a diverse set of trade and investment policies to meet the Japanese automotive challenge. Through the 'Elements of Consensus' and related understandings, the Community imposed limits on Japanese auto exports to the region as a whole and to five specific EC markets until the year 2000. In addition, through these arrangements the Community effectively constrained the operation of Japanese transplants within the region and linked levels of output at these transplants to overall permissible levels of Japanese auto exports bound for the EC.[50] Finally, individual European states such as Great Britain exacted 'voluntary' minimum local content pledges from Japanese auto firms in exchange for various financial incentives.

The United States also received large increases in Japanese automotive FDI during the 1980s, although the entry of Japanese car companies in America generally preceded their entry into Europe. In 1982, for example, Honda manufactured its first car at the Marysville, Ohio plant the firm had set up some years earlier to produce motorcycles. Nissan began turning out autos from its Smyrna, Tennessee factory in 1983, and Toyota began making the Chevrolet Nova in Fremont, California together with joint venture partner General Motors the following year. These direct Japanese investments in the US auto industry were followed by those of Mazda in Flat Rock, Michigan (1987), Mitsubishi Motors in Normal,

Illinois (1988), and a wholly Toyota-owned transplant factory in Georgetown, Kentucky (also in 1988). The Toyota investment in Kentucky alone reportedly amounted to some $1.1 billion by the end of the decade.[51]

Although the United States as well as Europe received massive inflows of Japanese FDI into the automobile sector, American policy responses to such Japanese investments contrast markedly with analogous European responses. Rising Japanese car exports to the United States first led Washington to negotiate a voluntary export restraint agreement. This agreement, announced in 1981, placed limits on the numbers of Japanese automobiles and certain other kinds of motor vehicles exported to the American market for a period of three years. Following a one-year extension, however, the Reagan Administration terminated this bilateral arrangement in 1985, although for essentially political reasons the Japanese government continued to limit auto exports to the United States for almost a decade thereafter.[52]

Yet the imposition of these trade controls, which partially explains the subsequent development of Japanese FDI in the US auto industry, was not followed by investment controls on Japan's American transplant factories. Indeed, the United States government did not seek to impede the entry or in general to impose performance requirements on the operation of Japanese automobile factories in the United States.[53] Instead, individual American states actively vied with each other to lure Japanese auto companies to their locales. The state of Kentucky, for example, 'won' Toyota by providing the Japanese company with some $350 million in incentives, including funds for site preparation, new roads, job training, and land acquisition, to locate its planned American transplant factory in that state.[54] Other US states provided substantial financial incentives to induce Japanese auto transplant investments by Honda, Nissan, Mazda, and Mitsubishi Motors.[55] Yet, in offering such incentives, these American states did not insist on exacting British-style local content pledges nor in general impose any other performance requirements on Japanese auto firms.[56]

America, like Europe, confronted a Japanese automotive challenge, yet the policy responses of governments in these two recipient regions differed in highly significant ways. With respect to trade, the Europeans insisted on major export controls on Japanese cars until the year 2000, whereas the Americans dropped such controls years earlier. And with respect to investment, the Europeans effectively imposed export and other restrictions on Japanese transplant factories, whereas the Americans permitted the entry and operation of Japanese auto transplants generally free of such encumbrances.

NOTES

1. Portions of this chapter, in an earlier version, were published in Mark Mason, 'Elements of Consensus: Europe's Response to the Japanese Automotive Challenge,' *Journal of Common Market Studies*, 32: 4 (Dec. 1994), 433–53, and in id., 'The Political Economy of Japanese Automobile Investment in Europe,' in Mark Mason and Dennis Encarnation (eds.), *Does Ownership Matter? Japanese Multinationals in Europe* (Oxford: Oxford University Press, 1994), ch. 11.
2. Commission of the European Communities, *Panorama of EC Industry, 1991–1992* (Luxembourg: Office of Publications of the European Communities), 13–19.
3. On the substantive but also symbolic importance of the automobile industry to France, for example, see Jean-Pierre Lehmann, 'France, Japan, Europe and Industrial Competition: The Automotive Case,' *International Affairs*, 68: 1 (1992), 44.
4. *New York Times*, Aug. 12, 1991. Stated limits in the accord refer to 1999, although in practice these limits also apparently refer to intervening years. See below.
5. This analysis of the 1991 EC–Japan automobile accord and related arrangements is based in part on copies of the original agreements made available to the author.
6. Although the 1991 accord also deals with certain categories of trucks, this analysis will focus exclusively on the automobile industry.
7. For background on the development of the European automobile industry see, in particular, Daniel T. Jones, *Maturity and Crisis in the European Car Industry: Structural Change and Public Policy* (Brighton: Sussex European Research Centre, 1981); Stephen Young, 'European Car Industry,' in Klaus Macharzina and Wolfgang H. Staehle (eds.), *European Approaches to International Management* (New York: Walter de Gruyter, 1986), 147–62.
8. IMVP World Assembly Plant Survey, as cited in Steven Tolliday, 'Globalization or Regionalization: The European Automobile Industry Faces 1992,' Harvard Business School Case No. 9-391-207.
9. Daniel T. Jones, 'The Competitive Outlook for the European Motor Vehicle

Industry,' *International Journal of Vehicle Design*, 11: 3 (1990), 222–33; id., 'A Second Look at the European Motor Industry,' working paper, IMVP International Policy Forum, May 1989; John Krafcik, 'European Manufacturing Practice in a World Perspective,' working paper, IMVP International Policy Forum, May 1988; IMVP World Assembly Plant Survey, as cited in Tolliday, 'Globalization or Regionalization'; and James P. Womack, 'The European Motor Industry in a World Context: Some Strategic Dilemmas,' working paper, IMVP International Policy Forum, May 1988.

10. For further explication of Calvet's views see, in particular, Jacques Calvet, 'Thank God for Quotas' (interview), *European Affairs* (Dec. 1, 1991), 68–71; and 'Preparing for the 1990's: PSA Aims to be Number One in the EC,' *JAMA Forum*, 8: 1 (Sept. 1989), 8–13.

11. Leading managers at the European subsidiaries of Ford and General Motors, motivated in part by their interpretations of the American experience with Japanese automotive competition in the United States, generally supported the positions of those calling for greater European protection.

12. Well after completion of the 1992 program, British Aerospace sold the Rover Group to German automaker BMW. This led Honda and Rover to terminate their equity relations, but various cooperative projects between the two firms continued. See, for example, *Financial Times*, June 13, 1994.

13. Nissan Jidosha, *Jidosha sangyo handobukku* (Automobile industry handbook) (Tokyo: Nissan Motor Company, 1990 edn.), 12–13.

14. Ibid.

15. These new, quantitative restrictions supplemented operative tariffs in the Community. Indeed, major European countries such as France, West Germany, Great Britain, and Italy all maintained separate (and high) tariffs on auto imports throughout the 1950s and early 1960s. By 1967, the six initial members of the European Economic Community had agreed to a common external automotive tariff of 17.6%, a rate which would fall in subsequent years (and which additional countries would eventually adopt after they had joined the Community). On the development of European public policies towards the automobile industry see, in particular, Jones, *Maturity and Crisis in the European Car Industry*; Étienne de Banville and Jean-Jacques Chanaron, *Vers un système automobile européen* (Towards a European automobile system) (Paris: Economica, 1991).

16. On the workings of the French system, which limited import penetration by placing percentage caps on annual Japanese car registrations, see Didier Salvadori, 'The Automobile Industry,' in Henry P. Bowen et al., *The European Challenge: Industry's Response to the 1992 Programme* (London: Harvester Wheatsheaf, 1991), 62–3.

17. This treaty was imposed on the Italians by Japanese officials, who feared large imports of small, competitive Italian automobiles. In exchange for agreeing to limit Italian car exports to Japan, Italy obtained the right to

limit Japanese car imports to Italy. See Salvadori, 'The Automobile Industry,' 63.

18. The precise nature of the German arrangement with Japan remains controversial. The most commonly accepted version of that arrangement holds that the two sides came to a gentleman's agreement during a visit of Otto Lamsdorf to Tokyo in 1981—the same year that the US and Japan settled on an auto restraint arrangement. The German–Japanese agreement, according to this account of events, specified a 15% Japanese auto import ceiling. Other versions suggest that Japan agreed to limit increases of its exports to Germany to no more than 1% per year, or that the understanding began in 1985 rather than 1981.

19. This system operated throughout the 1980s under a special DG IV announcement. During subsequent bargaining, the Commission at times sought to use the threat of discontinuing this derogation when disagreements arose with certain member states.

20. Commission data, as cited in *Financial Times*, Sept. 26, 1991.

21. The French government, on the other hand, once again demonstrated its long-standing ambivalence towards FDI in France's auto industry. This attitude led the French to reject, among other Japanese FDI proposals, Subaru's plan to establish a motor vehicle plant in Tours in 1988.

22. On the Nissan entry into the UK see, in particular, Peter Dicken, 'Japanese Penetration of the European Automobile Industry: The Arrival of Nissan in the United Kingdom,' *Tijdschrift voor Econ. en Soc. Geografie*, 78: 2 (1987), 94–107.

23. Toyota, the last of the major Japanese carmakers to establish a UK manufacturing plant, raced to produce its first automobile in that plant before completion of the internal market. This Toyota accomplished on December 16, 1992—just sixteen days before the formal opening of the new EC market! On Toyota's initial run, see *Financial Times*, Dec. 17, 1992.

24. Member states effectively blocked imports of Japanese cars from other EC states by invoking Article 115 of the Treaty of Rome. Article 115 generally allows the Commission, in the event of certain economic difficulties, to authorize member states to enact protective measures against foreign competitors. However, in case of 'urgency' during the 'transitional period,' member states *themselves* retain the sovereign right to implement such measures. After 1992, however, member states would lose the right unilaterally to invoke Article 115 against Japanese auto imports from other EC countries.

25. A preliminary (and highly publicized) skirmish took place in 1988, when French authorities threatened to block imports of Nissan Bluebirds assembled and partially manufactured in the UK. See, for example, *The Economist*, Oct. 8, 1988. The French finally relented, but the affair underlined the extraordinary sensitivity of the issue.

26. For an early attempt to assess EC policy options in the auto industry as unification approached, see Gianfranco Viesti and Laura Zanzottera, 'Japanese Multinationals and EEC: The Case of [the] Car Industry,' Working Paper No. 30, Centro Studi sui Processi de Internazionalizzazione, Universita Bocconi (Milan, Nov. 1989).

27. Resolutions adopted by the EC Parliament regularly urged adoption of a tough policy line against the Japanese car industry in Europe, but the Parliament apparently had little direct impact on the negotiations.

28. The following account necessarily simplifies an extraordinarily complex process. Within the Community itself, for example, a multiplicity of interactions took place between the Commission, member states, and firms. On the general nature of such interactions see, for example, Susan Strange, *States and Markets* (London: Pinter, 1988).

29. The Commission also consulted with MITI. However, the Japanese remained largely peripheral during these initial consultations, and did not become directly involved until the start of intensive Commission–MITI talks in January 1990.

30. Some of these states did, however, host limited foreign-controlled assembly operations, or were home to certain automobile parts suppliers.

31. The following account is drawn largely from the author's interviews with principals and others involved in this process, together with the account provided by Thierry Gandillot in his *La Dernière Bataille de l'automobile européenne* (The last battle of the European automobile) (Paris: Fayard, 1992).

32. Bangemann apparently excluded Peugeot chairman Jacques Calvet because the French car manager proved exceptionally severe in his stance towards the Japanese. Instead, BMW management was invited to attend.

33. On Hahn's revised thinking, see, for example, Bernard Avishai, 'A European Platform for Global Competition: An Interview with VW's Carl Hahn,' *Harvard Business Review* (July–Aug. 1991), 103–13. Indeed, the growing success of Japan's luxury car lines, such as the Accord (Honda), the Infiniti (Nissan), and the Lexus (Toyota), would soon encourage even Germany's specialist makers to shift quietly towards this harder line.

34. The European subsidiaries of Ford and General Motors were also granted full membership in the ACEA, a position denied them in the CCMC.

35. On May 8, 1991, the Permanent Representatives of the twelve EC members met to consider the revised Commission proposals. Even in its revised form, however, the proposed agreement remained too controversial for the adoption of a formal negotiating mandate. Therefore, when the Council of Ministers met on May 13, the automobile question was removed from the agenda. Gandillot, *La Dernière Bataille*, 136.

36. Chief among these outstanding issues was any mention in the accord of

reciprocal European access to the Japanese automobile market, a measure advocated from time to time by EC hardliners.

37. This internal French discord was also played out within the nation's auto industry: the impasse between Industry Minister Farroux and Prime Minister Cresson mirrored the split between Renault's Levy and Peugeot's Calvet. In the end, of course, the authorities tilted towards the more conciliatory line of (state-owned) Renault.

38. Under the final terms, this bilateral consensus—which forecast a significant *contraction* of the 1993 EC auto market—reportedly led MITI to agree to *reduce* Japanese motor vehicle exports to the Community by 9.3% during the 1993 calendar year. See *Financial Times*, Apr. 2, 1993. The following year, however, marked growing disagreements between the two sides over appropriate export levels. See, for example, 'Japan to Press EU over Vehicle Imports,' *Financial Times*, Sept. 9, 1994.

39. Representatives of Toyota and Nissan reportedly told Commissioner Andriessen during the course of the negotiations that it was the practice of their companies to sell in *local markets* those cars they produced in overseas subsidiaries. Commission officials interpreted this statement as a subtle form of assurance that Japan's two major carmakers would not export to the EC cars produced in their US transplant factories. However, no written understanding about this issue was ever produced.

40. Experience to date suggests that the Commission will classify as 'American' imports into the Community those Japanese-badged cars produced in the United States which the American authorities assert are 'American.' *Automotive News*, various issues; and interview with Joseph Massey, formerly of the Office of the United States Trade Representative.

41. The EC–Japan agreement also leaves open the tantalizing question of how the Community will handle auto imports from other rising Asian competitors such as Hyundai of South Korea.

42. See, for example, Calvet interview in *Nihon keizai shimbun*, Oct. 25, 1991.

43. *Nihon keizai shimbun*, Aug. 2, 1991.

44. Ibid., Aug. 1, 1991.

45. As quoted in *The Times* (London), July 28, 1991.

46. As quoted in *New York Times*, Aug. 12, 1991.

47. Indeed, the Commission reportedly stated that it had in fact 'taken into account' expected 1993 EC sales from Japanese transplant factories in calculating 1993 limits on Japan's auto exports to the Community. See *Financial Times*, Apr. 2, 1993.

48. Horst Herke, GM Europe Vice-President for EC Relations, as cited in *Ward's Automotive International* (May 1992).

49. See, for example, James P. Womack and Daniel T. Jones, 'European Automotive Policy: Past, Present, and Future,' in Committee on Foreign Affairs, US House of Representatives, *Europe and the United States: Competition and*

Cooperation in the 1990's (June 1992), 209. A renewal of EC protections from 2000 would be consistent with what Fiat Chairman Agnelli predicted in 1989 would likely turn into 'a kind of permanent negotiation' between the Community and Japan. See 'Agnelli on Cars, Greens, and Japan,' *Fortune* (July 31, 1989), 133, 136.

50. In addition, the 'Elements' and related understandings may well represent the first major example among such countries in which restrictions are based on the nationality of the producer rather than the location of production.

51. Mira Wilkins, 'Japanese Multinationals in the United States: Continuity and Change, 1879–1990,' *Business History Review* 64 (Winter 1990).

52. The Japanese government terminated its auto export restraints to the United States on March 31, 1994. *New York Times*, Mar. 29, 1994.

53. According to one former US government official, however, on at least one occasion in the early 1990s, American officials, in auto talks with their Japanese counterparts, did express the desire that Japanese auto transplants in North America increase auto parts purchases from US-based auto parts suppliers. Comments of Edward Lincoln.

54. Martin Kenney and Richard Florida, *Beyond Mass Production: The Japanese System and its Transfer to the US* (New York: Oxford University Press, 1993), 295.

55. Ibid.

56. Although concluding in general that in the United States 'there is not much economically important restriction of FDI at the state and local level in the manufacturing sector,' Graham and Krugman do raise the possibility that local governments in the United States at times may have elicited informal pledges from Japanese and other foreign companies to provide 'certain local benefits' in a limited number of cases. Edward Graham and Paul Krugman, *Foreign Direct Investment in the United States* (3rd edn., Washington, D. C.: Institute for International Economics, 1995), 141. Even if true, however, available evidence suggests that such cases were the exception rather than the rule. This contrasts sharply, of course, with the widespread imposition of such FDI controls in Europe, often applied as a matter of national policy affecting all incoming investors in a particular sector.

3

Consumer Electronics

IN addition to the automotive sector, manufacturing firms based in Japan also expanded aggressively into the European consumer electronics industry. A number of leading Japanese multinationals in this sector had set up modest European marketing, sales, and distribution operations by the late 1960s, as previously noted, but direct investments in regional manufacturing plants remained minuscule and overall FDI levels in this sector quite modest. Japanese direct manufacturing investment in the European color television industry from the 1970s represented that Asian nation's first significant expansion via FDI into Europe's broader consumer electronics sector, but Japan's great investment surge into this sector would not occur until the latter half of the following decade.

As in the automobile sector, the nature of the European public response to successive economic contests with Japan in various segments of the consumer electronics industry naturally carried important implications for the entire region. European production of consumer electronics, for example, was valued at some 40 billion ecu in 1991, and directly employed tens of thousands of workers.[1] Indeed, by the late 1980s consumer electronics accounted for roughly 25 per cent of the value-added of the Community's entire electronics industry.

To examine the nature of European policies in this sector, this chapter analyzes the Community's responses towards a number of major instances of the Japanese consumer electronics challenge. To place this analysis in context, critical aspects of the European consumer electronics industry are first outlined. Next, this chapter explores the character of Japanese strategies and European policies in three key sectors of the industry in which Japan invested heavily: color televisions, videocassette recorders, and compact disc players. Finally, the chapter contrasts European and American policy approaches towards Japanese competition in this sector.

THE EUROPEAN CONSUMER ELECTRONICS
INDUSTRY

The consumer electronics industry comprises a diverse and changing group of audio-visual products. Largely dominated by the color television segment in the 1960s, the industry later produced a number of other major products including video equipment such as videocassette recorders, video cameras and camcorders, audio equipment such as hi-fi and compact disc players, and related items. Relative market saturation for many of these products had contributed to a temporary slowdown in the growth of various segments of the industry in the early 1990s, yet newly emergent products offered the prospect of renewed growth as the decade progressed.

In Europe, this industry had long been divided among numerous firms operating in fragmented national markets in which governments often played important roles. Commonly operating within small, protected economies, Europe's traditional consumer electronics firms manufactured in relatively small plants which impeded scale economies and other benefits which could accrue to larger, more integrated producers. Indeed, the United Kingdom alone was host to no less than ten color television manufacturers— eight British-, one American-, and one Dutch-owned—as late as 1967.[2] Similar fragmentation and inefficiency also characterized many other major consumer electronics markets such as that of the former West Germany.[3] Government intervention, which contributed mightily to the European industry's structural characteristics and evolutionary path, included not only public support and regulation of individual firms, but also outright public ownership, perhaps most notably in the case of Thomson of France.

Declining international competitiveness in many sectors caused major structural changes in the European industry. A report commissioned by the EC and published in 1985, for example, found that locally-owned firms in general were far less productive than their Japanese counterparts.[4] This lagging international competitiveness was evident in virtually all major product groups and all large European markets. These trends, together with the spectacular rise of the Japanese consumer electronics industry and the equally spectacular demise of the American industry, had led to global Japanese leadership with only a modest European presence and an even

TABLE 11. The world's top fifteen consumer electronics companies (1990)

Ranking	Company	Nationality	Turnover ($ billion)
1	Sony	Japanese	16.2
2	Matsushita	Japanese	16.0
3	Philips	Dutch	14.0
4	Toshiba	Japanese	10.4
5	Hitachi	Japanese	7.6
6	Mitsubishi Electric	Japanese	7.1
7	Thomson CE	French	6.1
8	JVC	Japanese	4.9
9	Pioneer	Japanese	3.9
10	Sanyo	Japanese	3.0
11	Grundig	German	2.6
12	Goldstar	South Korean	1.7
13	NEC	Japanese	1.7
14	Nokia	Finnish	1.7
15	Zenith	American	1.2

Note: Data reflect turnover as published in annual reports according to categories most closely related to consumer electronics. Matsushita figure includes JVC turnover.

Source: Data provided to the author by BIS Strategic Decisions.

TABLE 12. The global consumer electronics industry: production, trade, and consumption across the Triad (1988)

Country or region	Production	Imports	Exports	Trade balance	Total market	Import ratio (%)
Japan	32.2	0.7	16.8	+16.1	16.1	4.3
European Community	10.7	9.3	1.2	−8.1	18.8	49.5
United States	5.4	11.2	0.9	−10.3	15.7	71.3

Note: Figures in billions of dollars.

Source: Commission of the European Communities, *The European Electronics and Information Technology Industry: State of Play, Issues at Stake and Proposals for Action* (Brussels: Commission of the European Communities, 1991), 27.

weaker American position. (See Table 11 for a ranking of the world's top fifteen consumer electronics companies in 1990; see Table 12 for production, trade and consumption in this industry across the Triad in 1988.)

This Japanese challenge to the European consumer electronics industry encouraged widespread mergers, acquisitions, and other forms of restructuring in Europe principally during the 1980s. Philips, for example, took control of Grundig; Thomson acquired Telefunken, Nordmende, and Ferguson; and Nokia gained control of Oceanic and the German subsidiary of ITT. By the end of that decade, these three firms—Philips, Thomson, and Nokia—had emerged as the region's pre-eminent locally-based manufacturers. Together with numerous outright withdrawals by a variety of European producers, the European consumer electronics industry as a whole had become far more concentrated than in previous years.[5]

JAPANESE STRATEGIES, EUROPEAN POLICIES

Color Television

Color television (CTV) became a significant component of the modern European consumer electronics industry at a relatively early date, yet the local industry remained fragmented for many years thereafter. European-based electronics firms first began to manufacture CTVs in quantity in the 1960s, following development of the product in the United States after World War II. Despite the ensuing development of the CTV market across the European Community, however, as noted above for many years this sector remained highly fragmented.

Differing CTV transmission standards greatly contributed to the fragmentation of the European industry.[6] In the US, the Federal Communications Commission (FCC) adopted the so-called NTSC (National Television System Committee) standard for CTV in 1953, which the Japanese subsequently chose as well.[7] In Europe, however, the authorities debated the adoption of two other standards. Pointing to better image quality and other advantages, the French proposed European-wide adoption of its so-called SECAM (*séquence couleur à mémoire*) standard, whereas the West German company Telefunken advocated use of the PAL (phased alteration lines) standard which it had pioneered. Unable to reach agreement, France (and Greece) opted for the SECAM standard, whereas most other European countries chose PAL.[8] Since producing CTVs which could operate on both standards initially proved far too expensive,

European CTV production was effectively divided not only among various firms within each country, but also among different firms in each standards zone.

Although competitive Japanese firms potentially could capture significant shares of developing European CTV markets through exports, difficulties in obtaining access to requisite technologies for producing PAL-compatible sets and other hindrances effectively discouraged major Japanese competition. With respect to standards, for example, PAL patent holder Telefunken initially refused to license any Japanese producers. Later, in 1973, the German company agreed to provide such licenses to select Japanese firms, but laid down two important conditions: first, Telefunken demanded that these firms limit their exports of PAL-compatible CTVs to Europe; and second, they stipulated that such firms could not sell within the Community PAL-compatible CTV sets which were larger than 20 inches and which were manufactured outside the EC.[9] Furthermore, differing national tastes and preferences contributed to segmentation of EC markets which rendered Japanese penetration even more costly and time-consuming.[10]

In addition to these private-sector impediments, a variety of public controls also hindered Japanese CTV exports to the Community. At the regional level, for example, the Commission imposed a common 14 per cent EC tariff on all CTV imports. Moreover, individual EC states imposed a variety of their own restrictions. The French and Italians, for instance, both maintained national CTV import quotas.[11] And the British government in 1973 negotiated a voluntary export restraint (VER) arrangement which limited the Japanese share of the UK CTV market to just 10 per cent.[12] For these and related reasons, Japanese import penetration of Community CTV markets—unlike its earlier penetration of the US CTV market—increased only gradually beginning in the early 1970s.[13]

Such import barriers stimulated Japanese FDI in the European CTV industry. By the late 1960s, Japanese electronics firms already had greatly increased their direct investments in European-based distribution and sales outlets to enhance their export efforts.[14] Starting in the early 1970s, however, these firms also began to establish CTV manufacturing facilities in Europe. Sony was the first Japanese company to build such a European plant when it set up a CTV factory in the UK in 1973. Sony's decision was quickly followed by

TABLE 13. Japanese FDI in the UK color television industry (1990)

Year	Company	No. of employees
1973	Sony	2,400
1974	Matsushita	1,475
1978	Hitachi	See Notes
1979	Mitsubishi Electric	514
1981	Toshiba	989
1982	Sanyo	600
1986	NEC	900
1987	Funai	280
1987	JVC	414

Notes: Hitachi (1978) investment represents joint venture with General Electric Company; Hitachi gained 100% ownership in 1984. Data on employees not available. Sony plant expanded in 1991.

Source: Data provided to author by Invest in Britain Bureau.

rival Matsushita, which also chose the UK as its plant site. These initial Japanese direct investments in the European CTV industry were followed by those of other Japanese companies starting later in the decade. Japanese firms concentrated their investments in the UK and West Germany, in large part to take advantage of the size of these markets and their use of the more widely adopted PAL standard.[15] (See Table 13 for the development of Japanese FDI in the UK CTV industry.) Japanese companies in general chose to manufacture the locally popular large-screen CTVs in their European plants because, as noted above, they were banned from importing them under the PAL license conditions.[16]

Yet just as earlier European restrictions hindered Japanese trade in CTVs, so later European restrictions constrained Japanese investment in this industry segment. In the critically important British market, for example, extra conditions attached to the original PAL licenses restricted exports from Japan's local CTV subsidiaries to no more than 50 per cent of total production.[17] In addition, in exchange for receiving official regional development grants and discretionary regional assistance, Sony, Matsushita, and other Japanese CTV producers in the UK were obliged by the British government rapidly to increase local content and to meet other performance requirements as well.[18] And, from 1977 until 1985, the British Department of Industry effectively blocked new greenfield investments by Japanese firms and required new investors to make specific local content commitments. These UK government controls forced Hitachi to enter the UK in 1978 by acquiring a 50 per cent stake in an existing General Electric Company venture and to accept other conditions as well.[19] Similar UK policies also led to the creation of a 70:30 Rank–Toshiba joint venture that same year.[20] The British had induced Japanese CTV firms to invest in order to avoid trade controls, yet such firms then confronted onerous investment regulations as well.[21]

As a result of these European policies, Japanese electronics firms rapidly localized their CTV manufacturing operations in the Community. Both Sony and Matsushita, for example, met their early 1970s commitments to the British government on local content levels, and later boosted those levels still higher. In addition, subsequent CTV manufacturing investments in the UK by other Japanese electronics firms likewise achieved high (at least 45 per cent) local content within specified periods of time.[22] British export requirements were also met by these Japanese firms. And many such firms then began transferring to their UK and other European operations increasing responsibility for R & D functions as well.[23]

At the same time, however, protectionist European policies and practices in part enabled European-owned firms to retain large shares of Community CTV markets. To be sure, many European CTV firms chose to leave the industry or were acquired by larger local competitors in the face of Japanese (and, later, particularly South Korean) competition. Nonetheless, three European consumer electronics firms—Philips, Thomson, and Nokia—together came to dominate all other local producers in this industry segment. (See Table 14 for EC CTV production capacity levels from 1984 to 1988.) At the same time, however, Philips and Thomson relocated significant proportions of their CTV production to Malaysia, Singapore, and elsewhere in East Asia.

TABLE 14. European color television production capacity (1984–1988) (thousands of units)

Firm	1984	1986	1988
Philips	3,050	3,100	3,400
Thomson	2,100	1,050	2,650
Nokia	500	680	2,250
Sony	310	535	850
Sanyo	—	150	700
Hitachi	200	370	500
Matsushita	230	300	400
Mitsubishi	95	125	200
Bang & Olufsen	130	145	150
Sharp	—	5	100

Source: Adapted from Alan Cawson and Peter Holmes, 'The New Consumer Electronics,' in Christopher Freeman, Margaret Sharp, and William Walker (eds.), *Technology and the Future of Europe: Global Competition and the Environment in the 1990s* (London: Pinter, 1991), 171.

Videocassette Recorders

Invented in the United States but never successfully commercialized there by American-based firms, the videocassette recorder (VCR) was initially introduced to European consumers by Philips. Together with the German firm Grundig, in which it then held a 25 per cent equity stake, Philips marketed the model N1500 in Europe in the early 1970s followed by the more advanced N1700 later in the decade. These products enabled Philips and its German partner to capture major shares of the German, British, Dutch, and other markets through 1977. Not yet seriously challenged by foreign competition, a local manufacturer had succeeded in staking out a central position in the small but rapidly growing European VCR industry.[24]

Despite Philips's early lead, however, Japanese competitors soon captured major shares of Community VCR markets. Already dominant at home and in the United States, Japanese firms next targeted Europe. In a critical strategic move designed to encourage general European adoption of its video home system (VHS) format over its rival Sony's Beta and the evolving Philips systems, Japan Victor

Company (JVC) in 1977 signed trade and production agreements with EC electronics firms based in each of the three major European VCR markets which had not allied with Philips or Grundig. In its agreements with Thorn EMI in the UK, Thomson in France, and Telefunken in West Germany, JVC forged original equipment manufacture (OEM) arrangements initially to export its VHS systems to Europe for sale under the Thorn, Thomson, and Telefunken brand names, and later to produce its VCRs jointly with these firms in Europe.

Already technically superior to the Philips machines and enjoying significant cost advantages thanks in large part to their huge scale economies realized through domination of their home and US markets, JVC and other Japanese makers dramatically increased their export penetration of the Community's VCR markets beginning in 1978. Philips and Grundig fought back with their 1981 introduction of the model V2000, but with little effect. Technical problems, initial tape shortages, and high production costs made this latest (and last) non-VHS-compatible VCR offered by these two EC firms no match for the increasing success of JVC and other Japanese VCR producers in Europe and elsewhere.[25] Indeed, between 1980 and 1981 Japan's production of VCRs doubled, and by 1982 Japanese manufacturers accounted for no less than 94 per cent of global VCR production.[26]

Rapid Japanese import penetration of the EC's VCR markets provoked strong trade restrictions at the national and Community levels. Some EC countries, such as Spain, opted to impose explicit quotas on imported Japanese VCRs.[27] Other countries, such as France, chose less explicit means. Fearful that Japanese import competition would exacerbate bilateral trade imbalances and determined to delay further VCR imports until enactment of a VCR import tax in 1983, the French government in late 1982 unilaterally restricted Japanese VCR imports by requiring that each imported machine undergo an arduous and time-consuming customs clearing procedure in the remote town of Poitiers. Only machines accompanied by instruction booklets written in French might eventually gain the requisite government import approvals.[28]

Rising Japanese import penetration also prompted Communitywide policy responses. After Philips and Grundig threatened to file an anti-dumping suit against allegedly offending Japanese VCR manufacturers—and with the backing of key member states—the

European Commission negotiated with Japan's Ministry of International Trade and Industry the Community's first-ever voluntary restraint agreement (VRA).[29] Under the terms of the agreement, the Japanese agreed to restrict VCR exports to the EC for three years beginning in 1983. In addition, this VRA set minimum prices which were pegged at levels designed to close the gap between Japanese and Philips VCR production costs. And finally, the agreement limited the numbers of unassembled VCR kits Japanese firms could export to recently established Japanese plants within the Community, which effectively operated as a local content requirement on such investments (see below).[30]

Yet European impediments to Japanese VCR imports did not stop there. Following expiration of the VRA accord at the end of 1985, for example, the Commission chose to raise the Community import tariff on VCRs from 8 to 14 per cent. Moreover, certain EC member states such as France apparently imposed informal national import quotas even after the termination of the 1983 accord. And signals from various member states encouraged the Japanese unilaterally to restrain VCR exports to the Community in subsequent years.[31]

As in the CTV experience, so in the VCR segment as well European trade controls encouraged Japanese direct investment. This investment entered Community markets in two successive waves. In the early- to mid-1980s, JVC, Sony, Matsushita, Hitachi, Sanyo, Mitsubishi, and Toshiba all established VCR manufacturing facilities within the EC. Two of these Japanese companies entered through joint ventures—JVC with Thorn EMI and AEG-Telefunken, and Matsushita with Bosch/Blaupunkt. Virtually all of these (and later) plants were located in either the UK or West Germany, and initially such subsidiaries sourced heavily from Japan and elsewhere outside the Community. A second wave of investments came in the late 1980s. Responding to renewed EC trade pressures, Funai and Orion in addition to NEC set up local VCR plants, and numerous Japanese firms which had entered earlier in the decade built additional plants or augmented their investments in existing Community manufacturing facilities.[32]

Also similar to the CTV case, European authorities placed major constraints on the local VCR investments of Japanese firms. As we have already seen, for example, provisions of the 1983 VRA imposed Community-wide limits on the importation of Japanese VCR kits to Community assembly plants, thereby forcing these plants to boost local sourcing. The Commission later imposed additional FDI

TABLE 15. The European videocassette recorder market: sales, local production, and Japanese imports (1982, 1985–1989) (millions of units)

Year	Total EC sales	Total EC production	Japanese share of total EC production	Japanese imports
1982	5.0	0.9	0.7	4.0
1985	5.4	2.2	1.7	3.1
1986	6.5	2.9	2.3	3.3
1987	8.2	4.2	3.0	3.5
1988	10.1	5.0	4.6	3.2
1989	11.1	6.2	5.6	3.6

Note: Non-Japanese imports principally from South Korea.

Source: Rene Belderbos, 'Strategic Trade Policy and Multinational Enterprises: Essays on Trade and Investment by Japanese Electronics Firms' (Ph.D. thesis, Erasmus University, Amsterdam, 1993).

constraints following its 1987 decision to amend Community antidumping legislation. Under the revised measures, the Commission could apply anti-dumping penalties to VCRs produced at certain Japanese-owned EC assembly plants which did not source at least 40 per cent of their parts from local suppliers.[33] The Commission then imposed just such penalties on locally produced VCRs of various Japanese operations.[34] Such regional controls were supplemented with national restrictions such as France's informal local content requirements on the Akai VCR plant located within its borders, and informal British requirements which forced Japanese VCR firms to attain minimum 45 per cent local content levels at their UK manufacturing facilities.[35]

These European FDI controls encouraged Japanese VCR makers to localize their EC operations rapidly. As early as 1984, for example, most Japanese VCR plants in the EC had attained 25 per cent local content levels, and by that date some had even reached 40 per cent levels. Moreover, virtually all plants had reached 45 per cent levels by the mid-1980s, and some had achieved still higher levels of local sourcing. This rapid localization of VCR production in the EC in turn enabled Japanese firms to capture overwhelming shares of Community markets largely through local value-added activities rather than exports from Japan or other non-Community locations (see Table 15).[36]

TABLE 16. Japanese videocassette recorder exports: US versus EC shares (1981–1988)

Year	Total exports (thousands of units)	Percentages of total		
		US	EC	Other
1981	7,355	32.0	38.8	28.9
1982	10,652	24.0	46.4	30.1
1983	15,237	35.7	30.5	33.8
1984	22,071	53.9	17.0	29.1
1985	25,475	62.5	12.8	24.7
1986	27,689	65.0	10.9	24.1
1987	22,801	54.3	12.7	33.0
1988	22,039	43.4	15.1	41.5

Source: Official Japanese data as cited in Laura Tyson, *Who's Bashing Whom? Trade Conflict in High-Technology Industries* (Washington: Institute for International Economics, 1992), 236.

Although European-owned firms in the VCR industry failed to maintain significant shares of local markets, through national and Community policies the EC managed to create a notably different set of outcomes from those in the United States. Overwhelming Japanese competitive strength largely forced European holdout Philips in 1985 to abandon its attempt to popularize its own VCR format, and in subsequent years the Dutch firm joined other producers in the Community by adopting the JVC-patented VHS system instead. Thereafter, European markets were largely dominated by Japanese manufacturers as well as EC-owned producers operating under Japanese license. In contrast to the United States, however, in the European Community local VCR markets were largely supplied through the local value-added activities of Japanese and other firms rather than through imports from outside the region. (See Table 16 for Japanese VCR exports to the US versus the EC from 1981 to 1988.)

Compact Disc Players

Dutch inventor Philips pursued a very different strategy in commercializing the compact disc (CD) player as compared with its strategy to expand the European market for its VCR machines. Indeed, the Dutch firm was determined that it would not repeat the mistakes over format standards it had committed in the VCR contest. Accordingly, after fellow European producer Thomson declined to enter into joint efforts to develop a commercially viable CD player, Philips approached Sony about collaborating in further development of the product.[37] Sony, like Philips a loser to VHS in the VCR format wars, agreed to cooperate in such development and in the creation of a single standard for the new product.[38]

The CD player proved extremely popular with consumers, and Philips initially captured major shares of European markets. The product was first introduced into the marketplace in 1981, and new increases in consumer penetration from 1982 soon made the CD player what one expert termed 'the most successful product in consumer electronics history.'[39] To supply the burgeoning European market, Philips set up a single factory in Belgium in an effort to centralize production and exploit scale economies. Thanks to these and other factors, in the mid-1980s the Dutch company managed to capture major shares of Community markets for a product whose sales had reached some $3 billion worldwide in 1991, by which time the CD player had become a key component of the entire industry.[40] Despite the product's significant and growing importance, however, Philips was alone among European companies in manufacturing the CD player.

As with VCRs, so with CD players as well Japanese electronics companies quickly penetrated European markets through aggressive export drives. Pursuing a strategy to make their co-developed CD player standard throughout the industry, Philips and Sony licensed the technology to virtually every electronics firm which sought to obtain it. Although this action led to the universal adoption of the Philips–Sony standard, it also enabled all the major Japanese electronics companies to manufacture and compete in the CD player market from a relatively early date. With this new technology in hand, an increasing number of Japanese electronics companies together expanded their nation's production at prodigious rates beginning in 1982.[41]

Exports from Japan quickly followed. Between 1984 and 1987, for example, Japanese CD player exports worldwide increased by a factor of no less than 14, and such exports would continue to rise through the early 1990s (see Table 17).[42] Almost half of these exports

TABLE 17. Japanese CD players: production and exports (1983–1991) (tens of thousands of units)

Year	Production	Exports
1983	25	—
1984	77	54
1985	414	305
1986	736	603
1987	732	711
1988	932	921
1989	1,018	805
1990	1,092	914
1991	1,285	1,142

Source: Official Japanese data as cited in Dempa Publications, *Japan Electronics Almanac '93/'94* (Tokyo: Dempa Publications, 1993), 120.

TABLE 18. Japanese CD players: top five export markets (1990)

Rank	Country	Units (thousands)	Share (%)
1	US	4,955	45.4
2	Belgium	580	5.3
3	Germany	573	5.2
4	Taiwan	557	5.1
5	Hong Kong	535	4.9

Source: Dempa Publications, *Denshi kogyo nenkan 1993* (Electronics industry almanac 1993) (Tokyo: Dempa Publications, 1993), 663.

went to the United States, and elsewhere outside Europe as well Japanese firms dominated world markets. (See Table 18 for the top five destinations for Japanese CD player exports in 1990.) By contrast, Philips managed to maintain a significant position in the European CD player market, but from the early 1980s that position became increasingly eroded by rising rates of Japanese export penetration.[43]

In seeking to stem the flow of Japanese CD player imports into the Community, the Commission employed trade tools by now familiar to European governments and Japanese multinationals alike. Anticipating an early Japanese challenge in this new product segment, Philips and its member state backers successfully lobbied the Commission to institute a special 19 per cent tariff on imported CD players from 1983. The rate of this tariff steadily declined, to 16.5 per cent in 1987 and 9.5 per cent two years later, but was soon followed by an even stiffer import impediment.[44] Alleging that Japanese firms were now dumping CD players on EC markets, in mid-1987 the Commission launched an extensive anti-dumping investigation against these (and certain South Korean) firms.[45] This investigation led to the imposition of tentative import duties ranging up to 34 per cent in the summer of 1989, and to final duties ranging from 8 to 32 per cent in January 1990.[46]

The former of these Community actions had little influence on the location of Japan's production of CD players, but imposition of the latter (cumulative) import duty decisively altered Japanese strategies. In the earliest years of the industry, Japanese firms supplied EC markets entirely through exports from non-EC locations. When the Commission formally decided to initiate its anti-dumping investigation in 1987, however, Japanese electronics firms began to directly invest for the first time in EC-based CD player manufacturing facilities. Indeed, between 1987 and 1990 no less than ten Japanese multinationals together established eleven such operations in the Community. Unlike their location decisions in the CTV and VCR industries, however, Japanese firms opted to set up five of these eleven EC plants in France—with just one in the UK—due to major French national import quotas, comparatively high French market prices for consumer electronics products, and other factors.[47] This strategic shift to Europe contributed importantly to the global increase in Japanese offshore production of CD players in the late 1980s (see Table 19).

Once located within the Community, however, Japanese electronics firms confronted many of the same FDI controls in producing and selling CD players they had faced in the CTV and VCR industries. At the Community level, for example, informal regulations encouraged Japanese CD player manufacturers to attain at least 45 per cent local content levels in their EC factories. Moreover, understandings between individual Japanese producers and certain EC states such as France obliged these companies to increase local content levels still higher within specific periods of time. In addi-

TABLE 19. Japanese CD players: overseas production (1985–1990)

Year	Units (thousands)	Percentage increase over previous year
1985	2	—
1986	75	3,750
1987	386	515
1988	1,298	336
1989	3,488	269
1990	5,243	150

Source: Dempa Publications, *Denshi kogyo nenkan 1993* (Electronics industry almanac 1993) (Tokyo: Dempa Publications, 1993), 670.

tion, the French government, for example, apparently extracted concessions from Japanese producers that they would fulfill agreed levels of exports from their French factories over specified periods of time.[48]

This series of Japanese strategies and European responses in the CD player industry did produce certain outcomes which contrasted with those of the CTV and VCR cases, yet in all three examples the similarities are more striking than the differences. Unlike the CTV case, in CD players just one European-owned firm engaged in production and managed to retain a significant share (roughly 35 per cent in the late 1980s) of Community markets.[49] And unlike the VCR case, in CD players Philips managed to standardize in Europe (and elsewhere) the technical format which it had developed and championed.

Yet in all three industries, European policies significantly influenced not only the pattern of Japanese trade but also the development and character of Japanese investment as well. In each case rising Japanese exports prompted European trade controls, which in turn spurred Japanese direct investment and the subsequent imposition of European FDI constraints. These evolving interactions then induced Japanese firms to engage in full manufacturing operations in Europe, and thereby partially replace exports with local production.

EUROPE, AMERICA, AND THE JAPANESE
CONSUMER ELECTRONICS CHALLENGE

Europe confronted a series of major Japanese challenges in the consumer electronics industry. The first significant contest came in the CTV segment, where Japanese firms began to expand directly into Europe beginning in the 1970s. This was followed by Japanese FDI in other key segments of the European industry such as VCRs and CD players in the 1980s.

In seeking to meet each of these successive challenges, European officials applied major controls on Japanese firms in the region. In CTVs, for example, policy measures included the imposition of tariffs and quotas on Japanese imports together with the later adoption of local content and other performance requirements on the operation of Japanese direct investments in the Community. These and other trade and investment controls were later imposed on Japanese firms seeking to increase their penetration of the region's VCR and CD player markets as well.[50]

These policies contrast significantly with those adopted by the Americans in confronting their own Japanese Challenge in consumer electronics. Japan's first direct investments in this sector in the United States, as in Europe, entered the CTV industry. Anticipating later surges of Japanese FDI in a number of key industries, during the 1970s virtually all of Japan's major consumer electronics firms invested in US-based CTV manufacturing plants. In 1972, for example, just one year before its CTV direct investment in the UK, Sony opened its first US CTV factory in California. This was followed by Matsushita's direct investment in a manufacturing plant in Illinois (in 1974), Sanyo's in Arkansas (1977), Toshiba's in Tennessee (1978), Sharp's also in Tennessee (1979), and Hitachi's in California (1979). These investments were followed by subsequent large-scale Japanese FDI in this and other sectors of the consumer electronics industry during the 1980s. Indeed, in the latter half of the 1980s alone more than fifty Japanese electronics firms directly invested in Oregon alone.[51]

Despite the large-scale entry of Japanese consumer electronics firms in the United States and Europe, Japan's two Triad partners adopted very different policy approaches in response. In Europe, as we have seen, officials acted first to restrict imports by Japanese consumer electronics firms and then to control the European manufacturing operations of these firms undertaken in large part to avoid these trade restrictions.

America, by contrast, took a different policy approach. As Japanese exports to the United States of various consumer electronics products increased, American officials often did intervene to control these trade flows. With respect to the CTV sector, for example, the US Treasury Department imposed anti-dumping duties of up to 60 per cent on Japanese CTV imports as early as 1971, and in 1977 the United States and Japan reached an Orderly Marketing Arrangement to limit Japanese CTV exports to America.[52] However, in subsequent years the United States government did not directly impede the ensuing entry or operation of Japanese FDI in the CTV or other major sectors of the American consumer electronics industry, nor indirectly influence the competitive opportunities of Japanese subsidiaries operating in the United States through subsidies or other financial support to the dwindling number of locally controlled firms.[53] Indeed, as in the case of Japanese FDI in the US automobile industry, official US neutrality at the national level was often complemented by active encouragement of Japanese consumer electronics investments at the state level. Yet unlike individual European governments, American states generally did not then impose performance requirements on such investments.

NOTES

1. Commission of the European Communities, *Panorama of EC Industry 93* (Luxembourg: Office of Publications of the European Communities), 10–28.
2. Alan Cawson, Kevin Morgan, Douglas Webber, Peter Holmes, and Anne Stevens, *Hostile Brothers: Competition and Closure in the European Electronics Industry* (Oxford: Clarendon Press, 1990), 233.
3. See, for example, ibid., 289.
4. Boos, Allen & Hamilton, Inc., 'EEC Consumer Electronics Industry—Industrial Policy: Final Report', Brussels, June 24, 1985, unpublished.
5. Alan Cawson and Peter Holmes, 'The New Consumer Electronics,' in Christopher Freeman, Margaret Sharp, and William Walker (eds.), *Technology and the Future of Europe: Global Competition and the Environment in the 1990s* (London: Pinter, 1991), 170.

6. Cawson et al., *Hostile Brothers*, 233; 'Zenith and High-Definition Television,' Harvard Business School Case No. 9-391-084.

7. The NTSC had earlier developed with the FCC the original standard for black-and-white TVs. The American standard for CTVs was based on this original standard.

8. The French subsequently licensed the SECAM standard to the USSR and to countries of Eastern Europe in addition to Greece and many former French colonies. See Mackintosh International Ltd., *The European Consumer Electronics Industry* (Luxembourg: Office for Official Publications of the European Communities, 1985), part 4.

9. Cawson et al., *Hostile Brothers*, 224; Harvard Business School, 'Zenith and High-Definition Television.' The Japanese finally convinced Telefunken to modify its position under threat of exporting to Europe high-quality (300-line), low-cost CTVs not subject to the PAL patent. See Harry P. Bowen, 'Consumer Electronics,' in Harry P. Bowen et al., *The European Challenge: Industry's Response to the 1992 Programme* (London: Harvester Wheatsheaf, 1991), 260.

10. Unlike Americans, for example, in the early 1970s most Europeans still preferred larger-size TV screens. This raised transportation costs and therefore lowered potential profit margins. Bowen, 'Consumer Electronics,' 260.

11. Rene Belderbos, 'The Globalisation of Japanese Electronics Firms: Foreign Investment in the European Community,' in Frédérique Sachwald (ed.), *Direct Investment as a Modality of Globalisation: The Case of Euro-Japanese Relations* (Paris: Masson/IFRI, 1993), 10; Cawson et al., *Hostile Brothers*, 274; Laura D'Andrea Tyson, *Who's Bashing Whom? Trade Conflict in High Technology Industries* (Washington: Institute for International Economics, 1993), 241.

12. Michael Brech and Margaret Sharp, *Inward Investment: Policy Options for the United Kingdom* (London: Routledge & Kegan Paul, 1984), 64.

13. Bowen, 'Consumer Electronics,' 260; Belderbos, 'The Globalisation of Japanese Electronics Firms,' 19.

14. See Ch. 1 and Brech and Sharp, *Inward Investment*, 68.

15. Cawson et al., *Hostile Brothers*, 245, 249–50; Brech and Sharp, *Inward Investment*, 68.

16. Brech and Sharp, *Inward Investment*, 69.

17. This condition applied to Japanese production of PAL-compatible CTVs anywhere in the EC. See Cawson et al., *Hostile Brothers*, 245.

18. Ibid.

19. Ibid., 222; IBB data. Moreover, British authorities had earlier rejected a proposed Hitachi greenfield investment despite the Japanese company's promises to source locally 70% of its components and export 50% of its production. Cawson et al., *Hostile Brothers*, 243–4, 250.

20. Cawson et al., *Hostile Brothers*, 249.

21. Yet these British FDI policies were mild in comparison with those of the French, whose general hostility to virtually all Japanese FDI until 1982, together with the local use of the SECAM standard, discouraged any Japanese CTV FDI in France. Ibid., 268.
22. Tyson, *Who's Bashing Whom?*, 241.
23. See, for example, Belderbos, 'The Globalisation of Japanese Electronics Firms,' 30–1, table 17.
24. Cawson et al., *Hostile Brothers*, 225, 255; Tyson, *Who's Bashing Whom?*, 221.
25. Mackintosh International Ltd., *The European Consumer Electronics Industry*, 79. In 1983, for example, the V2000 captured just 8% of the British VCR market, whereas VHS held 70% and Beta the remaining 22%. Cawson et al., *Hostile Brothers*, 256.
26. Cawson et al., *Hostile Brothers*, 226–7.
27. Belderbos, 'The Globalisation of Japanese Electronics Firms,' 12.
28. Cawson et al., *Hostile Brothers*, 282.
29. The motivations of key member states to support the call for a VRA were varied. The British, for example, apparently believed that such an arrangement would encourage still greater inflows of Japanese FDI to their home market; the French favored the accord because they thought it would further their concurrent efforts to create a 'European champion' in VCRs through official encouragement for Thomson to acquire Philips-allied Grundig; and the Germans chose to acquiesce to the wishes of their British and French counterparts under strong pressure from their domestic consumer electronics firms. Cawson et al., *Hostile Brothers*, 290; Tyson, *Who's Bashing Whom?*, 222.
30. Cawson et al., *Hostile Brothers*, 257; Tyson, *Who's Bashing Whom?*, 224.
31. Cawson et al., *Hostile Brothers*, 282, 312.
32. Belderbos, 'The Globalisation of Japanese Electronics Firms,' 11–12, and tables 3, 10, and figure 3; Tyson, *Who's Bashing Whom?*, 228; Cawson et al., *Hostile Brothers*, 230, 312.
33. Technically, these plants were required to source at least 40% of their components from non-Japanese sources. According to Rene Belderbos, however, in practice Japanese firms felt obliged through this requirement to source from EC suppliers. Rene Belderbos, *Strategic Trade Policy and Multinational Enterprises: Essays on Trade and Investment by Japanese Electronics Firms* (Amsterdam: Timbergen Institute, 1994), 39.
34. Vulnerable Japanese companies were those which had previously been penalized for dumping imported VCRs in the Community. See Belderbos, 'The Globalisation of Japanese Electronics Firms,' 12–13; Tyson, *Who's Bashing Whom?*, 228–30.
35. Indeed, at least one account suggests that the Community as a whole imposed informal 45% local content requirements on local Japanese VCR plants. See Kenneth Flamm, 'Semiconductors,' in Gary Hufbauer (ed.),

Europe 1992: An American Perspective (Washington: Brookings Institution, 1990), 275 n. 74.

36. Belderbos, 'The Globalisation of Japanese Electronics Firms.'

37. Contact between the two firms was initiated by an executive of the German firm Grundig, who advocated wide-ranging European cooperation with Japanese electronics firms as the best way to redress the bilateral EC–Japan trade imbalance. Internal Commission memorandum, Oct. 8, 1991.

38. Cawson et al., *Hostile Brothers*, 227–8, 338, 372; Cawson and Holmes, 'The New Consumer Electronics,' 179.

39. Cawson et al., *Hostile Brothers*, 339.

40. Ibid., 227–8; Bowen, 'Consumer Electronics,' 256–7.

41. EIAJ (Electronics Industry Association of Japan), *Denshi kogyo nenkan: 1993* (Electronics Industry Almanac), 719.

42. Ibid.

43. Bowen, 'Consumer Electronics', 262; Alan Cawson, 'European Consumer Electronics: Corporation Strategies and Public Policy,' in Margaret Sharp and Peter Holmes (eds.), *Strategies for New Technology: Case Studies from Britain and France* (London: Allan, 1989), 60.

44. Rene Belderbos, 'On the Advance of Japanese Electronics Multinationals in the EC: Companies, Trends and Trade Policy' (unpublished working paper, n.d.), 33; id., 'The Globalisation of Japanese Electronics Firms,' table 4.

45. Industrial Bank of Japan, *Special Report 131* (Tokyo: IBJ, n.d.), 58; Belderbos, 'The Globalisation of Japanese Electronics Firms,' table 4.

46. Belderbos, 'On the Advance of Japanese Electronics Multinationals,' 15; id., 'The Globalisation of Japanese Electronics Firms,' table 4. In addition, the Commission opted to start yet another round of anti-dumping investigations against Japanese (and South Korean) producers in mid-1992, alleging that these firms were attempting to circumvent existing EC anti-dumping duties by exporting their CD players via Taiwan, Singapore, and Malaysia. Reuters, June 12, 1992.

47. Belderbos, 'On the Advance of Japanese Electronics Multinationals,' 15–16; Cawson et al., *Hostile Brothers*, 230.

48. Belderbos, *Strategic Trade Policy and Multinational Enterprises*.

49. Cawson, 'European Consumer Electronics,' 60.

50. The Europeans also adopted measures to support locally controlled companies against Japanese competitors. In the CTV segment, for example, member states or the Community as a whole adopted the PAL or SECAM standards to provide advantages for local firms against their major Japanese competitors.

51. Japanese companies which invested in Oregon, some to exploit the advantages of that state's growing concentration of firms in the semiconductor as well as consumer electronics sectors in 'Silicon Forest,' included NEC, Fujitsu, Kyocera, Epson, and Sharp. Mira Wilkins, 'Japanese Multinationals

in the United States: Continuity and Change, 1879–1990,' *Business History Review*, 64 (Winter 1990).

52. Belderbos, *Strategic Trade Policy and Multinational Enterprises*, 45.

53. The earlier demise of large sectors of the US CTV and other consumer electronics sectors—brought about in part through intense competition from Japan—surely lessened whatever American industry pressure may have been applied on US policymakers to control Japanese FDI in the industry. On that demise, see MIT Commission on Industrial Productivity, 'The Decline of US Consumer Electronics Manufacturing: History, Hypotheses and Remedies,' in *Working Papers of the MIT Commission on Industrial Productivity* (Cambridge, Mass.: MIT Press, 1989), vol. i. In the *industrial* electronics sector, however, Fujitsu withdrew its 1987 bid to acquire 80% of Fairchild Semiconductor—then controlled by the French conglomerate Schlumberger—following opposition voiced in certain US business and government quarters. Yet this was an exceptional case, and the opposition was apparently based on the close relationship of Fairchild to the US Department of Defense as well as fears that the Fujitsu acquisition could lead to anti-trust violations in the US semiconductor industry. See Martin and Susan Tolchin, *Buying into America* (New York: Times Books, 1988), 12.

4

Banks

THE great surge of Japanese FDI in the late 1980s provoked powerful fears among many in the banking sector of the unifying European Community.[1] Already Japanese multinationals had mounted major challenges to EC automobile and consumer electronics manufacturers in Community markets. Next, warned some observers, Japanese competitors would aggressively penetrate EC banking and other financial services sectors. 'The principal Japanese financial organizations, which have pursued a policy of systematic expansion,' declared one French analyst in 1987, 'have literally invaded the markets and exacerbated competition between different banking groups.'[2] Moreover, a Belgian consultant that same year detected 'astonishing parallels' between earlier Japanese manufacturing successes and more recent Japanese efforts to 'dominate' the financial services industry in Europe and elsewhere. 'If the prospect of a Toyota in every garage frightened you,' he asked, 'what about a Nomura Securities office in every city and a Dai-Ichi Kangyo Bank on every corner?'[3]

This perceived Japanese banking challenge, combined with EC allegations that Japan did not grant adequate reciprocal access to Community banks, stimulated lively debates across the EC over the entry and operation of Japanese banks in the Community after completion of the Single Market. Until the end of 1992, of course, individual EC member states would retain the power to regulate the entry and operation of Japanese (and other foreign) banks in their home markets. Passage of the Single European Act, however, obliged all twelve EC nations to cede certain of these national powers to Community-wide bodies through implementation of common policies in the vitally important financial services sector beginning January 1, 1993.[4] Would the Community unconditionally grant Japan's banks non-discriminatory access to unified EC financial markets, or would it first require that Japan meet certain reciprocal standards of market access?

To explore these and related issues, this chapter examines in particular the creation of relevant portions of the Second Banking Coordination Directive (2BCD), the central piece of EC legislation which dealt not only with matters of internal financial integration, but also with the entry and operation of Japanese and other non-EC banks in the Community after 1992.[5] To place this analysis in proper context, the chapter will first examine certain salient characteristics of the EC banking industry together with the development of Japanese banks in Europe and evolving EC policy responses. Next, the process of crafting key provisions of the 2BCD as well as resulting outcomes and denouements will be examined. Finally, this chapter will compare and contrast European and American policies towards their respective Japanese banking challenges.

CONTEXT

The European Banking Industry

In at least two important respects, the character of the EC banking industry was marked by extraordinary diversity in the late 1980s. For one thing, the structure and performance of the industry varied widely between (and often within) member states. In structural terms, industry concentration as measured by the market shares of the top five banks by country in 1988 ranged from just 30 per cent in Luxembourg and 36 per cent in the United Kingdom to 84 per cent in the Netherlands and 83 per cent in Greece.[6] (See Table 20 for a list of the top twenty-five European banks, by capital, in 1988.) Moreover, the number of banks varied from some 751 in the UK to just 27 in Portugal by the end of 1986. (See Table 21.)

These and other factors created enormous disparities in the economic performance of the banking industry in individual EC countries.[7] As measured by assets per employee, for example, in 1984 the productivity of the Luxembourgeois industry exceeded that of the Danish industry by a factor of almost five.[8] Using these same indicators, the British, Germans, and Dutch in addition to the Luxembourgeois attained the highest levels of productivity in the Community, whereas the French, Spanish, and Greeks in addition to the Danish achieved among the lowest levels.[9] Differing levels of productivity, in turn, contributed to varying rates of profitability.

TABLE 20. The top twenty-five European banks, by capital (1988)

Bank name (location of parent)	Capital ($ m.)	Assets ($ m.)
National Westminster (UK)	10,907	178,505
Barclays (UK)	10,545	189,368
Crédit Agricole (France)	9,152	210,601
Union Bank of Switzerland (Switzerland)	6,715	110,760
Deutsche Bank (West Germany)	6,460	170,808
Swiss Bank Corporation (Switzerland)	6,055	102,466
Lloyds Bank (UK)	5,867	93,800
Banque Nationale de Paris (France)	5,567	196,955
Midland Bank (UK)	5,499	100,849
Crédit Lyonnais (France)	5,409	178,878
Paribas (France)	5,324	121,617
Société Générale (France)	4,874	145,661
Crédit Suisse (Switzerland)	4,785	75,388
Rabobank (Netherlands)	4,666	80,808
Groupe Écureuil (France)	4,372	150,253
Dresdner Bank (Germany)	4,284	129,733
Banco Bilbao Vizcaya (Spain)	4,138	63,340
Instituto Bancario S. Paolo (Italy)	4,075	103,105
Monte di Paschi di Siena (Italy)	3,625	66,560
Cariplo (Italy)	3,504	54,131
SE Banken (Sweden)	3,412	46,965
TSB Group (UK)	3,364	40,078
Banca Naz del Lavoro (Italy)	3,352	87,729
Banco Central (Spain)	3,200	40,659
Banca Commerziale Italiana (Italy)	3,178	62,700

Source: *Banker* (Oct. 1989), 76.

Thus it has been estimated that the pre-tax real rate of return on equity for the period 1984–6 ranged from a positive 18 per cent in the UK to a negative 17 per cent in Portugal.[10]

In addition to diverse structure and performance, the EC banking industry also was characterized by differing regulatory regimes imposed by individual member states.[11] In one important respect, of course, these countries followed a common regulatory policy towards their respective financial services industries. In the United States, the Glass–Steagall provisions of the Banking Act of 1933

T A B L E 21. EC banking systems: number of firms, by function and nationality (1986)

Country	No. of commercial banks	No. of savings and mutual banks	No. of foreign banks	No. of domestic banks
Belgium	86	31	61	56
Denmark	219		5	214
France	367	624	131	860
Germany	252	598	148	702
Greece	33	2	19	16
Ireland	42	17		59
Italy	200	85	38	247
Luxembourg	122		102	20
Netherlands	81	67	40	108
Portugal	27		9	18
Spain	136	213	36	313
UK	611	140	300	451

Note: The figures '219' for Denmark and '27' for Portugal refer to their respective combined numbers of commercial *and* savings and mutual banks.

Source: E. Baltensperger and J. Dermine, 'European Banking: Prudential and Regulatory Issues,' in J. Dermine (ed.), *European Banking in the 1990s* (Oxford: Basil Blackwell, 1990), 20–1.

mandated a strict separation of the banking and securities industries. This separation was also enforced in post-war Japan through implementation of Article 65 of the Securities and Exchange Act of 1947. By contrast, most European governments had long permitted firms to engage in both banking and securities (i.e. universal banking). This fundamental difference in regulatory approach between the EC and its two Triad partners would later create major difficulties as Europe contemplated external banking policies for the Single Market.

Nonetheless, important regulatory differences within the EC remained. The British, Dutch, German, and Luxembourgeois governments generally placed the fewest requirements on the entry and operation of banking institutions in their territories.[12] The United Kingdom, for example, had operated a system with relatively little government intervention from well before World War II.[13] The British authorities did impose or maintain various restrictions in the post-war period, yet in comparative international terms those restrictions were not terribly severe.[14]

By contrast, many other EC states imposed far stricter controls on their banking industries. The Belgian, French, Irish, and Italian governments, for example, all maintained foreign exchange controls through the late 1980s. Yet public authorities intervened still more heavily in the Greek, Portuguese, and Spanish industries. The Greek government, for example, controlled all interest rates, imposed sizeable reserve requirements, and strictly regulated capital flows; Portuguese officials regulated interest rates and maintained various credit ceilings and strict foreign exchange controls; and the Spanish state obliged local banks among other things to purchase low-interest-yielding government securities and to maintain unusually large reserves.[15]

Member states did agree to implement various common rules towards the banking industry following adoption in 1957 of the Treaty of Rome.[16] Notably, in June 1973 the European Council of Ministers adopted a directive calling upon member states to ensure that banks from other EC countries would enjoy national treatment with regard to entry and operation within their territories.[17] And in December 1977 the Council adopted the so-called First Banking Coordination Directive (1BCD), which, among other requirements, obliged member states to harmonize various types of banking regulations and established the basis for the principle of home country control.[18] Additional pieces of EC legislation in the banking field were subsequently adopted and generally implemented.

Despite these trends toward greater Community-wide banking regulation, however, individual member states managed to retain enormous powers over their domestic banking industries. Some states, such as France, successfully fought to maintain for many years their sovereignty over certain matters covered in the 1BCD by insisting on long transitional periods before operative clauses became binding on all member governments.[19] For these and other reasons, even after adoption of the 1BCD, banks based in other EC countries still had to obtain permission from host authorities to operate locally, remained subject to the supervision of those authorities, and were required to observe other regulations determined by host officials as well.[20] Indeed, according to one analyst, the harmonization program spelled out in the 1BCD and other Community initiatives 'largely failed as a result of the resistance of the Member States to relinquishing control over their banking institutions.'[21] New challenges would soon sharpen the debate over national versus Community powers to regulate the banking industry.

Japanese Strategies, European Policies

Japanese banks initially entered European markets in the late nineteenth century, as noted above, but their presence remained quite limited through the 1960s. The earliest entrant, the Yokohama Specie Bank, operated its first European representative office in London in the 1880s both to provide financial services to support Japan's burgeoning trade with Europe and to funnel foreign capital into the expanding Japanese economy. This entry also set a more general locational precedent, for many Japanese banks in succeeding decades would choose to base their European operations in the City of London. Nonetheless, between them a handful of Japanese banks such as Mitsui, Mitsubishi, and Sumitomo had established facilities in Berlin, Hamburg, and Paris in addition to London before World War II.[22]

The operation of Japanese banks in Europe resumed after the hiatus of war and occupation, but once again their presence was modest. During the 1950s, for example, Fuji, Teikoku, Mitsubishi, and Sumitomo Banks in addition to the Bank of Tokyo established limited operations in London. A number of other Japanese banks entered European markets in the 1960s and again generally opted to base their operations in the City, yet their size and the range of their activities likewise proved marginal.

European host governments have naturally influenced the local entry and operation of Japanese and all other foreign banks for more than a century, yet regulations imposed by the Japanese government at times have proved even more influential.[23] Indeed, the Japanese authorities strictly limited the overseas expansion of their nation's banks from at least the late nineteenth century, providing support for some but preventing or limiting the movement abroad of many others. In the post-war era, relevant controls were largely contained in provisions of the Banking Law, the Foreign Exchange and Foreign Trade Control Law (FEFTCL), and other measures, and all were administered by the Ministry of Finance (MOF). Japanese banks seeking to engage in foreign exchange transactions, for example, had to submit to rigorous, lengthy, and complex bureaucratic procedures under the FEFTCL before they could hope to obtain requisite permissions.[24]

Beginning in the 1970s, however, changing Japanese government regulations made possible the general expansion of Japanese banks into Europe. MOF gradually liberalized controls on the establishment of overseas branches and representative offices by Japanese banks during that decade, for example, but continued generally to prohibit lending in Japan to non-residents.[25] As demand for funds by oil-consuming nations increased dramatically in the early 1970s, Japanese banks therefore responded by establishing or expanding their London operations to act as booking centers for making loans to these nations. In addition, of course, increasing numbers of Japanese banks operated in London and elsewhere in Europe to provide financial services to Japanese industrial corporations shifting from exports to local manufacturing in the region.[26]

Japanese banks expanded far more aggressively in European markets during the 1980s, and here again changes in Japan's regulatory policies as well as important economic developments spurred this growth. With respect to Japanese regulation, the government's 1980 revision of the FEFTCL and other actions liberalized still further domestic controls on overseas expansion by banks based in Japan.[27] At the same time, there arose major new demands for funds which Japanese banks could most effectively meet through European-based operations. These demands initially included large American and European multinational borrowers in the Euromarkets, as well as the rapidly expanding demands of Japanese industrial corporations who themselves turned increasingly to the less regulated Euromarkets to raise funds.[28] And later, growing Japanese fears that EC unification might create a 'Fortress Europe' encouraged numerous Japanese banks to establish operations in EC markets both to service the financial needs of their Japanese clients' growing presence in Europe and to themselves establish local subsidiaries before stricter, Community-wide controls might be imposed.

As a result of these and many other developments, Japanese banks vastly increased their presence in the European financial services sector during the 1980s.[29] Between 1981 and 1988, for example, the value of Japanese bank assets in the United Kingdom more than tripled. (See Table 22.)[30] This rapid increase was part of a far

TABLE 22. Location of assets of Japanese banks ($ billion)

Year ending December:	Offices in Japan	Foreign branches		
		Total	UK	US
1981	791	233	134	74
1982	811	310	161	97
1983	980	350	178	108
1984	926	421	194	131
1985	1,339	600	257	151
1986	1,927	837	359	208
1987	2,854	1,090	426	252
1988	3,044	1,120	445	307

Source: H. Terrell, R. Dohner, and B. Lowrey, 'The Activities of Japanese Banks in the United Kingdom and in the United States, 1980–1988,' *Federal Reserve Bulletin*, 76: 2 (Feb. 1990), 40.

larger expansion of Japanese international bank assets during the 1980s, which by 1986 already had catapulted Japan far ahead of the United States into the top-ranking position in this category.[31] Such dynamic growth was also reflected in the relative asset positions of banks worldwide, which by 1988 included nine Japanese banks out of the top ten positions. (See Table 23.)

Japanese banks augmented their European operations during the 1980s through various forms of representation in an increasingly large number of EC locations. In contrast to their earlier expansion patterns in the Community which generally had begun with large increases in branches, Japanese banks greatly expanded their network of subsidiaries in the EC, starting in the mid-1970s but particularly in the early- to mid-1980s.[32] In addition, during the 1980s these banks broke a century-old pattern of concentrating their European presence in the UK and certain other northern countries whose financial systems were relatively less regulated by creating new operations in, most notably, France, Italy, and Spain.[33] As a result, although Japanese banks already in 1982 constituted the largest foreign bank group in London, no less than 31 Japanese banks

TABLE 23. The top ten banks in the world, by assets (1981 versus 1988)

	1981		1988	
	Bank	Country	Bank	Country
1	Citicorp	US	Dai-Ichi Kangyo	Japan
2	Bank of America	US	Sumitomo	Japan
3	Crédit Agricole	France	Fuji	Japan
4	Banque Nationale de Paris	France	Mitsubishi	Japan
5	Crédit Lyonnais	France	Sanwa	Japan
6	Société Générale	France	Industrial Bank of Japan	Japan
7	Barclays	UK	Norinchukin	Japan
8	Deutsche Bank	West Germany	Crédit Agricole	France
9	Natwest	UK	Tokai	Japan
10	Dai-Ichi Kangyo	Japan	Mitsubishi Trust	Japan

Note: Ranked by capital rather than assets, Japanese banks held six (rather than nine) of the top ten positions in 1988.
Source: *Banker* (July 1981), and (July 1989), 54.

together operated an estimated 51 branches and 22 subsidiaries in 8 different EC countries just five years later. (See Table 24.)[34]

This dramatic Japanese expansion into Europe, however, contrasted sharply with the relatively minor presence which European banks had managed to achieve in Japan.[35] In 1981, for example, the assets of all foreign banks in Japan amounted to just 2.5 per cent of total banking assets in that country. That small proportion of foreign as compared to total assets ranked Japan well below most EC countries. Indeed, Japan ranked not only below those EC states whose domestic markets were exceptionally open to the entry of foreign bank assets, such as Luxembourg (85.5 per cent of total assets), the UK (60.2 per cent), Belgium (48.6 per cent), and the Netherlands (18.0 per cent), but also below the domestic markets of other EC members whose markets remained relatively less open, such as those of France, Spain, and Germany.[36] Nor had the relatively meager presence of EC banks in Japan greatly expanded during the course of the 1980s. Thus, for example, in 1989 the assets

TABLE 24. Japanese banks in the European Community (1987)

Name of bank	UK	Belgium	W. Germany	Luxembourg	Netherlands	Spain	France	Italy
Bank of Tokyo	B	B	B (2)	S	S	B	B	B
Bank of Yokohama	B	S						
Chuo Trust and Banking	B							
Dai-Ichi Kangyo	B		B	S	S			
Dai-Ichi Europe	S							
Daiwa	B		B					
Daiwa Europe	S							
Fuji	B	B	B	S			B	
Hokkaido Takushoku	B	S						
Industrial Bank of Japan (International)	S							
Industrial Bank of Japan	B		B	S			B	
Kyowa	B				S			
Kyowa Finance International	S							
Long-Term Credit Bank of Japan (Nippon European Bank)	B	S						
Mitsubishi (Europe)	B	B	B			B		
Mitsubishi Trust and Banking	B							

TABLE 24. *Continued*

Name of bank	UK	Belgium	W. Germany	Luxembourg	Netherlands	Spain	France	Italy
Mitsui	B	B	B			B		
Mitsui Trust and Banking	B	S						
Nikko	S							
Nippon Credit	B							
Nomura Bank International	S							
Saitama (Europe)	B	S						
Sanwa	B	B	B					
Sumitomo	B	B	B	S		B		
Sumitomo Trust and Banking	B							
Taiyo Kobe	B	B	B	S				
Tokai	B		B		S			
Toyo Trust	B							
Yamaichi	S							
Yasuda Trust and Banking	B							
Zenshinren	B							
Branches	24	7	12	0	0	4	3	1
Subsidiaries	7	5	0	6	4	0	0	0
TOTAL	31	12	12	6	4	4	3	1

Notes: 'B' denotes branch; 'S' denotes subsidiary.

Source: Adapted from *Banker* (Apr. 1988), 57–62.

of all foreign banks in Japan amounted to just 3.36 per cent of total assets, and all EC banks together held a mere 1.93 per cent of total assets in Japan. Many other measures of banking presence similarly point up the relatively minor position held by EC banks in Japan as compared to the positions of Japanese banks in most EC countries in the late 1980s.[37]

This large imbalance in overseas penetration by EC as opposed to Japanese banks in their reciprocal markets, together with the continued rapid expansion of Japan's banks in the EC and earlier examples of Japanese success in entering European manufacturing industries, provoked rancorous policy debates within the unifying European Community. In the past, as previously noted, individual member states had crafted their own policies towards foreign banks in their domestic markets. Alleging that Japan unfairly denied many of their financial services firms reasonable access to domestic markets, during the mid-1980s many EC countries unilaterally imposed reciprocity conditions on Japan. In 1985, for example, the French government blocked all new Japanese applications for securities licenses to operate in Paris until Japan agreed to permit Paribas and Société Générale to establish banking operations in Tokyo.[38] And in 1988, the British government refused to permit a single Japanese regional bank to open a branch or subsidiary in London until the Japanese authorities allowed two UK securities firms to apply for seats on the Tokyo Stock Exchange.[39]

Under the terms of the SEA, however, member states pledged to implement common policies by January 1, 1993 to achieve far greater financial integration within the Community. A chief tenet of the planned integration program was adoption of the so-called Single License, which would provide banks with at least one subsidiary in the EC freedom to establish operations and provide services throughout the Community. Under this system, officials and others asked, what conditions, if any, should Japan and other non-EC countries be required to meet before banks based in those countries could enjoy the full privileges of the Single License? And, further, who should create and implement any such conditions—the European Commission or individual member states? Questions such as these led the Bank of Tokyo to term the expansion of Japanese banks in Europe and elsewhere one of the 'issues of our time.'[40] Few responsible officials in the Community during the late 1980s were inclined to disagree.

THE SECOND BANKING COORDINATION DIRECTIVE

Process

The banking challenge from Japan encouraged the European Commission initially to propose tough Community-wide regulations on Japanese (and other non-EC) banks after completion of the Single Market. These regulations were spelled out in the first draft of the critically important 2BCD, which would become the principal EC legislative vehicle to meet the various financial integration goals set forth in the SEA.[41] Officials from the Commission's Directorate-General for Financial Institutions and Company Law (DG XV), the functionally responsible unit within the Commission, initiated the process by drafting in December 1987 third-country regulations for the proposed 2BCD, and presenting those regulations to the Council in February 1988.[42]

The Commission's initial proposals advocated a forceful and relatively uncompromising policy towards Japanese and other non-EC banks. In their draft, DG XV officials specified that a member state would be required to notify the Commission each time a non-EC bank requested authorization to establish a subsidiary or acquire participation in an operating Community bank in such a state.[43] The Commission then would examine within three months of receiving such notification how banks from all member states were treated in the home country of the non-EC bank, during which time the request of this bank would automatically be suspended. If the Commission found that all EC banks received reciprocal access in that third country, the concerned member state then could itself decide whether to approve the application. If, on the other hand, the Commission found that one or more EC banks did not enjoy reciprocal access in that third country, the Commission could extend the period of the suspension and submit proposals to the Council of Ministers to achieve reciprocity.[44]

This draft directive, which explicitly accorded substantial central powers to the Commission in overseeing this case-by-case application of reciprocity to non-Community banks, nonetheless failed to clarify at least two important matters. First, nowhere in the proposal was the precise meaning of reciprocity defined. And second, the proposal did not indicate whether the reciprocity clauses would in any way apply to previously established subsidiaries of non-EC banks in the Community.[45]

Although the Commission's proposal therefore contained a number of vague or ambiguous points, the principal aim of the reciprocity measure was clearly directed at Japan. 'The Japanese rightly suspect that they are the real target of the Commission's efforts,' reported the *Financial Times* in one lead editorial.[46] Indeed, interviews with responsible EC officials confirm this and similar reports. 'Japan was in our minds,' recalled, for example, one of the chief Commission architects of the reciprocity provisions in the proposed directive. In addition to the great influx of Japanese banks in the Community during the 1980s, he asserted, 'we believed that the Japanese financial services market was hermetically sealed.' Therefore, in drafting the proposed measures, 'Japan was our main target.'[47]

Revelation of the third-party clauses in the 2BCD provoked strong protests from non-Community groups. Japanese government officials and bank managers first expressed concern and then issued thinly veiled warnings as they pondered the implications of the proposed legislation. 'There were strong fears among Japanese banks that the EC was trying to impose a strict reciprocity rule,' recalled, for example, the President of the Mitsubishi Bank (Europe), 'which would be applied to Japanese banks already operating in the Community.'[48] 'It will work as a disadvantage to both the world economy and the EC itself,' warned the Managing Director of the Industrial Bank of Japan, 'if the concept of reciprocity is excessively pursued.'[49] At least one bank manager ventured still further. 'If Japanese banks were forced to close in the EC, then French banks and English banks in Tokyo would have to close,' predicted the Managing Director of the Sumitomo Bank in London. 'It would be like the Second World War.'[50]

Although the Commission had targeted the Japanese above all others in drafting its tough reciprocity measures, the United States protested the loudest. Fearing that the Commission might use the proposed directive as a means to enable EC banks to practice universal banking in the US by threatening sharply to curtail the operations of US banks in the EC, American business managers, government officials, and others quickly proved themselves the most outspoken foreign critics of the proposed EC regulations.[51] 'The American Chamber of Commerce (UK) believes strongly that the EC should be open,' proclaimed that organization's President, for example, 'and that the reciprocity conditions run counter to that aim. I feel that this issue is of utmost importance,' he went on, 'and warrants the attention of industry, business and government leaders.'[52] And Federal Reserve Governor Robert Heller, among other US officials, openly warned the Community that the incorporation of reciprocity in EC-wide policies could provoke a strong official American response.[53]

These and other external reactions stimulated spirited exchanges throughout the Community over the proposed regulations. Many powerful interests strongly supported the Commission's tough stance on reciprocity, particularly as a means of dealing with Japan. Some of the most ardent supporters of the Commission initiative represented business or government interests in EC countries whose banks in general were relatively less competitive and whose financial markets in general were relatively more regulated than their regional neighbors. Declarations in the European Parliament often advocated a particularly tough stance. 'Reciprocity is not a new notion—it is as old as international trade itself,' proclaimed one official before the Parliament. 'If I had to give a definition of reciprocity . . . I would say "It's a fair deal, it's a balance of benefits and obligations, a balance of profits and charges". . . . Certain third countries [i.e. Japan],' this official concluded, 'already have more than 15% of Community financial markets whereas we have scarcely 1% of theirs. This is not a "fair deal," this is not a balanced situation.'[54] Representatives of the French, Greek, Italian, and Spanish governments among others, as well as managers of various banks based largely in these countries, generally proved most vehement in their remarks.[55] A tough policy of reciprocity, they argued, was the most effective means of opening to EC banks those financial markets such as Japan's which they condemned as unfairly closed.[56]

Many other members of the EC banking industry equally favored Community efforts to prize open Japanese financial markets, but feared that strong reciprocity measures ultimately might jeopardize access to just such markets. The position articulated by the Banking Federation of the European Community, the trade group which represented the interests of banks throughout the EC, typified this modified approach. 'The inclusion of a reciprocity clause in EC Banking Regulations may be effective in stimulating the necessary change within those countries that currently discriminate against foreign banks, either overtly by law or regulation, or tacitly by market or administrative practice,' President Jeremy Morse of the Federation wrote to EC Commissioner Leon Brittan in the midst of the debates. Yet Morse also worried that a definition of reciprocity which effectively rendered it a 'blunt instrument' could provoke third countries into enacting like policies inimical to the interests of EC banks operating in those countries. 'The Federation [thus] strongly recommends a pragmatic and cautious approach regarding the application of the reciprocity requirement,' he concluded, 'to avoid charges of protectionism and the real danger of any retaliatory measures by third countries.'[57] At roughly the same time, however, the Federation issued a report particularly critical of alleged restrictions on foreign firms in Japanese financial markets.[58]

The strongest internal EC criticism against the proposed Commission measures, however, came from member states with large and established positions as international financial centers. These states, led by the UK and Luxembourg, felt most threatened by regulations which could bar the entry and operation of banks from countries such as Japan if the Commission found that even one EC-based bank faced unfair discrimination in those countries.[59] 'This proposal would erect a wall of protectionism round Europe and threaten London's position as one of the key financial centers in the world markets,' warned, for instance, the then UK Trade Secretary Lord Young. 'We oppose and we oppose strongly the reciprocity provisions of the [Second] Banking Directive.'[60] The UK among other member states already had the national authority to impose reciprocity conditions through provisions built into their domestic banking regulations, but opposed the creation of supranational powers with such authority wielded by the Commission. 'The UK is arguing strongly against a centralized reciprocity policy administered from Brussels,' reported the *Financial Times* in the midst of the debates. 'It believes each country should be free to administer it itself.'[61]

These Community debates over reciprocity greatly influenced the ultimate character of the EC's external banking policy as set forth in the 2BCD. In response to criticism that the proposed directive was overly protectionist, many Commission officials contended that the real intent of the reciprocity measures was to force open foreign financial markets rather than to close those based in Europe. 'The reciprocity clause has a positive liberalization goal,' argued, for example, one of the chief architects of the initial Commission plan, 'the liberalization of the international financial system as a whole.' [62]

However, the outright opposition of the governments of some powerful EC member states, together with the qualified opposition of various banking interests based in these and other such states, ultimately forced the Commission, in April 1989, to present to the Council significant modifications to its original reciprocity proposals.[63] These revised regulations were then discussed and approved by the Council that July, debated by the Parliament throughout the following autumn, and incorporated in the final version of the 2BCD which was officially adopted on December 15, 1989.[64]

Outcome

The Community's policy towards Japanese and other third-country banks as set forth in the final version of the 2BCD, which became effective on January 1, 1993, did indeed represent an important modification of the Commission's initial proposals.[65] First, the final version sought to define reciprocity by setting out two general standards.[66] One standard was whether a third country grants EC banks 'effective market access' comparable to what the EC grants banks from that third country. The other standard was whether EC banks enjoy 'national treatment' in a third country *with the same competitive opportunities as banks based in that country*. This de facto definition of 'national treatment' was apparently crafted with the allegedly subtle, extra-legal complications of the Japanese market in mind. The notion of 'effective market access,' designed to address still subtler forms of discrimination, again was developed largely in response to allegedly more transparent barriers in the Japanese case.[67] Still, by defining reciprocity according to these two standards, the Community implicitly ruled out the sterner test of mirror reciprocity in judging EC bank access to third countries (see Appendix II).[68]

The final version of the 2BCD significantly altered other aspects of the Commission's original proposal as well. In contrast to the procedures set forth in that proposal, the revised measures stipulated neither automatic suspension each time a non-EC bank applied to set up a subsidiary in the Community nor individual tests for third-country reciprocity in each such case. Rather, the 2BCD charged the Commission with undertaking systematic analyses of the treatment of EC banks in third countries at least six months before the January 1, 1993 implementation of the directive and periodically thereafter.

These analyses then determined the course of the application process. If the Commission found that EC banks did indeed enjoy both 'effective market access' and de facto 'national treatment' in the relevant third country, the member state to which the non-EC bank had applied for approval to establish a subsidiary could decide on the application without any automatic suspension imposed by the Commission. Third-country failure to meet either of the two reciprocity tests, however, would lead to very different results. If the Commission found that EC banks did not enjoy 'effective market access' in the relevant third country, the Commission could request from the Council a mandate for negotiation to seek a satisfactory change in the competitive opportunities for EC banks in that country.[69]

If, moreover, the Commission found that EC banks enjoyed neither de facto 'national treatment' nor 'effective market access' in the relevant third country, the Commission could on its own initiative open negotiations with that country to remedy the problem.[70] At the same time, but only with the approval of the Council obtained through a complex procedure, the Commission could also require the member state to which the concerned non-EC bank applied to limit or suspend for up to three months decisions on applications from that bank or other banks based in that third country. Any further limitations or suspensions beyond the initial three months, however, had to be initiated and expressly authorized by the Council. Finally, the revised 2BCD included a 'grandfather' clause which exempted third-country subsidiaries previously established in the EC from any sanctions imposed through this procedure.[71] This measure was particularly important for Japan, many of whose banks had consciously set up EC subsidiaries to avoid possible difficulties after the 2BCD took effect.

Despite these modifications, the revised 2BCD empowered the Community to impose substantial conditions on the entry of Japanese and other non-EC banks in Community financial markets. For one thing, the Community had set out important criteria for third countries whose banks might seek permission to set up local subsidiaries. Failure to meet the lesser of these two standards, de facto 'national treatment,' could result in temporary blockage of the requests of such banks on the initiative of the Commission, and indefinite blockage at the insistence of the Council. In addition, the vaguely defined notions of 'national treatment' and 'effective market access' granted the Community considerable discretion to judge the true openness of third countries such as Japan, and to place substantial pressure on such countries to modify conditions if the Community found that adequate reciprocal access did not obtain.[72]

At the same time, however, the final version of the 2BCD effectively granted member states continued powers to regulate the entry and operation of third-country banks even after completion of the Single Market.[73] Member states retained these powers for a number of important reasons. First, the reciprocity standards merely represented minimum conditions which third countries had to meet in order that their banks not encounter resistance to establish subsidiaries at the Community level. However, member states still retained the sovereign right under domestic regulation to reject applications of non-EC banks to establish local subsidiaries. Indeed, many of these domestic regulations specifically included reciprocity provisions. The UK, France, Greece, Ireland, the Netherlands, and Spain, for example, all had reciprocity clauses in domestic legislation concerning the establishment of both subsidiaries and branches, and member states Denmark, Germany, and Italy had legislation which enabled their governments to subject the local establishment of foreign branches to reciprocity standards. Moreover, according to a 1992 Commission report, 'some Member States, such as France, Greece, [the] Netherlands and the United Kingdom, have in their legislation provisions which enable them to impose other restrictions on the operation of foreign banks and financial companies, or to deny them certain benefits, if the country of origin of the firm discriminates against its firms or does not offer them competitive opportunities equivalent to those offered by these Member States to foreign banks and financial institutions.'[74] Finally, certain member states exercised additional rights to limit foreign participation in domestic financial markets through invocation of 'economic needs' and other criteria.[75]

Second, the final form of the 2BCD granted the (member-state controlled) Council the right to reject Commission proposals to impose suspensions or limitations whenever the 'national treatment' test was not met and to decide upon any extension of such suspensions or limitations.[76] Third, this Community banking legislation was in the form of a directive rather than a regulation. Thus, the 2BCD merely required that each member state modify domestic legislation to achieve the results set forth in the 2BCD, but did not specify the means which had to be adopted to achieve those results. 'The implementation of this legislation, and any additional measures which may be considered necessary in specific market conditions, is left in the hands of competent national authorities,' Commissioner Brittan thus rightly emphasized. 'This is right on grounds of subsidiarity—the principle that functions should not be centralized unnecessarily—but also for the very practical reason that only national supervisors have the capacity to control their own markets and market players effectively.'[77]

Fourth, member states may well employ various informal means to prevent, among other actions, third-country acquisition of domestic banks which they wish to maintain under local control.[78] And finally, although the Single License granted locally-established subsidiaries of third-country banks the general right to set up banking branches throughout the Community, still, each member state retains the right to regulate and supervise the operations of these and all other branches of third-country banks in the same way they do every other local bank branch.[79]

Denouements

Based on the 2BCD requirement to examine the environment for EC banks in third countries, the Commission carried out an extensive analysis of the Japanese financial services market in early 1992. The resulting Commission report, officially released that June, found that EC banks did indeed confront serious difficulties in the Japanese market. The chief problem cited, of course, was the strict separation of banking, securities, and insurance activities.[80] The Commission also noted, however, the existence of numerous additional impediments which either had been reported in the recent past or appeared to remain currently operative. These included such 'institutional' factors as inter-corporate shareholdings, which rendered foreign acquisitions of Japanese banks difficult. In addition, the Commission found that difficulties arose from 'administrative guidance' with respect to, for example, new product approvals. Also problematic were certain 'behavioral' features of the Japanese market such as 'the nature of business relationships' between Japan's banks and commercial firms, which rendered foreign access to potential clients especially challenging. Finally, the Commission noted in its report the lack of transparency concerning various governmental procedures.[81]

Despite these findings, however, the Commission concluded that, overall, Japan did in fact provide for EC and other foreign financial institutions de facto 'national treatment' with respect to both entry and operation. Although the authors of the 1992 report stated that a number of serious difficulties continued to hinder EC bank access to Japanese markets, they also asserted that most of these difficulties stemmed from various 'non-discriminatory features' of those markets. In addition, the Commission authors noted, Japan's Ministry of Finance was already engaged in a thoroughgoing liberalization of the financial services sector, which led them to conclude that 'many of the outstanding problems' confronting EC banks and other financial institutions 'are expected to disappear or diminish considerably.'[82] This 1992 report therefore recommended implicitly that the Community take no action against potential Japanese entrants into EC financial markets when the 2BCD would initially come into effect.[83]

Indeed, current trends suggest that the Community will not impose special restrictions on either the entry or operation of Japanese banks in the foreseeable future. In addition to the Commission's 1992 findings on the Japanese environment for EC banks, the vaunted Japanese challenge in banking appeared noticeably less menacing by the time the 2BCD had come into effect. Difficulties attributed to the dramatic decline in the value of Japanese real estate and corporate stocks, implementation of the Basle accords on capital adequacy, widespread financial scandals, and other factors all have contributed to major difficulties at many major Japanese banks in recent years. Such factors have in turn diminished considerably the European perception of the Japanese Banking Challenge.[84] Moreover, in July 1995 the Community agreed to participate in a new multilateral accord to further liberalize global financial markets. As a consequence, the Community chose to suspend the reciprocity clause of the 2BCD from mid-1996 through 1997.[85]

Whether or not the Community will in fact impose new restrictions on Japanese banks at some later date, however, will depend in part on the development of the Japanese environment for EC banks. Though current trends in Japanese financial liberalization offer hopeful signs, stated a leading DG XV official after the 2BCD formally took effect, 'our liberal policy cannot last forever.'[86] Nor was this official alone among Commission representatives in holding out the possibility of future action. 'If we find that our system provides firms from a third country with greater opportunities than European firms obtain in that country,' proclaimed, for example, Commissioner Brittan during a 1992 speech in Tokyo to the Institute for Financial Affairs, 'we regard ourselves as fully entitled to negotiate a more equitable balance of opportunities.'[87] Although Brittan took a prominent lead in negotiating the 1995 accord which led to the temporary suspension of the 2BCD reciprocity clause, just three years earlier he pointedly suggested that the Community might alter its current policies by restricting the operations of Japanese banks and other financial services firms already established in the EC if alleged Japanese discrimination against EC firms were to persist for too long.[88]

EUROPE, AMERICA, AND THE JAPANESE BANKING CHALLENGE

The Japanese Banking Challenge stimulated major policy debates across the European Community. Japan's competitive strengths in the automobile and consumer electronics industries raised fears among many Europeans that Japanese firms operating in the banking sector also might threaten local business and economic interests. These fears were magnified by the large and relatively sudden expansion of Japanese banks in many Community markets. Added to these fears of Japanese competition in Europe were allegations that Japan unfairly limited the entry and operation of EC banks in Japan.

For these and other reasons, the European Community fashioned a distinctive policy approach to the Japanese Banking Challenge in anticipation of the Single Market. Passage of the 2BCD constituted the most critical aspect of the EC response. This response provided for the flexible imposition of legal safeguards covering investment to protect EC financial markets in the event that Japan failed to offer EC banks adequate reciprocal access to Japanese markets. Member states, of course, also retained the right to impose various regulatory requirements on Japanese (and all other non-EC) banks even after completion of the Single Market.[89] Later developments did lead the EC temporarily to suspend this reciprocity clause, yet the clause remains in the Directive and the Community retains the right to reimpose this regulation at a later time.

Here again, however, European and American policy responses differed. Japanese banks aggressively expanded into the United States, as they did in Europe, following the 1980 revision of Japan's Foreign Exchange and Foreign Trade Control Law. California attracted particularly great interest. In 1983, for example, Mitsubishi Bank acquired the parent company of the Bank of California, and the California arm of the Bank of Tokyo took over California First Bank in 1987 and its extensive state-wide branch network, followed by its acquisition of Union Bank in 1988. By then Mitsui, Tokai, Dai-Ichi Kangyo, Sumitomo, and Sanwa Banks in addition to Mitsubishi Bank, the Bank of Tokyo, and other Japanese institutions all had directly invested large sums in California where they operated full-service banking operations. Indeed, by 1989 ten leading Japanese banks in California operated more than 400 branches, and Japanese banks as a whole controlled an estimated 25 per cent of the state's banking market.[90] Yet Japanese banks also entered financial services markets in other key states such as New York and Illinois, and by 1990 Japanese banks held over one-half of all foreign-owned bank assets in the United States.[91]

Despite the rapid expansion of Japanese banks in America, the United States adopted a policy approach different from that of Europe. Like all countries, of course, the United States regulates the establishment and operation of foreign- (and domestically-) controlled banks. At the federal level, the McFadden Act and the Bank Holding Company Act restrict multistate branching and certain categories of interstate bank acquisitions, for example, and the Glass–Steagall Act mandates strict separation of the banking and securities businesses. In addition, some American states by law prohibit foreign banks in particular from establishing branches or agencies in their jurisdictions, and all states ultimately retain wide-ranging discretionary authority to regulate financial institutions.[92]

In contrast to Europe, however, the United States government did not adopt regulations involving reciprocity standards in response to rapid inroads of Japanese banks to domestic markets. It is true that some in the US Congress, in 1990 and subsequently, proposed legislation empowering the Executive Branch to limit access to US markets by Japanese or other foreign-based banks whose home countries discriminated against or denied national treatment to US-based financial institutions. Yet Congress did not pass such legislation during the years of the Japanese Banking Challenge, but instead generally continued to grant Japanese (and other foreign-based) banks unconditional national treatment.[93] In addition, at the state level such major financial centers as California, Illinois, and New York maintained relatively open regulatory regimes which enabled large numbers of Japanese banks to expand their US operations rapidly into a number of different banking fields.[94]

In short, European authorities adopted new, reciprocity-based regulations at the Community level whereas the US government adopted no such reciprocity standards as the Japanese Banking Challenge gathered momentum. In addition, individual EC member states maintained major controls at the national level, whereas American states home to the nation's most important financial centers retained relatively open policy regimes towards Japanese banks throughout this period. In banking as in automobiles and consumer electronics, therefore, European policymakers chose more restrictive measures than their US counterparts in response to this Japanese Challenge.

NOTES

1. Portions of this chapter, in an earlier version, were published in Mark Mason, 'Europe and the Japanese Banking Challenge,' *Journal of Public Policy*, 13: 3 (Spring 1994), 255–78.
2. Jean-Marie Kertudo, 'L'Omniprésence japonaise' (The Japanese omnipresence), *La Revue banque*, 471 (Apr. 1987), 398.
3. This Belgian analyst was joined in his account of Japanese financial services by an American colleague. See Richard W. Wright and Gunter A. Pauli, *The Second Wave: Japan's Global Assault on Financial Services* (New York: St Martin's Press, 1987), 2–3.

4. Two summary statistics suggest the importance of financial services to the EC. In 1989, it was estimated that this sector accounted for some 7.4% of total Community output (measured in gross value-added at market prices), and about 4.7% of total Community employment. See Commission of the European Communities, Directorate-General for Financial Institutions and Company Law, 'Treatment Accorded in Third Countries to Community Credit Institutions and Insurance Companies: Report by the Commission to the Council,' mimeo (Brussels, June 22, 1992), 10. See, also, relevant portions of Commission of the European Communities, 'The Economics of 1992,' *European Economy*, 35 (Mar. 1988).

5. Second Council Directive of 15 Dec. 1989 on the coordination of laws, regulations, and administrative provisions relating to the taking up and pursuit of the business of credit institutions and amending Directive 77/780/EEC.

6. Data as cited in Damien Neven, 'Structural Adjustment in European Retail Banking: Some Views from Industrial Organization,' in Jean Dermine (ed.), *European Banking in the 1990s* (Oxford: Basil Blackwell, 1990), 171.

7. Analysis of the relative performance of EC banks and banking systems is, of course, highly problematic. The precise figures presented in the following discussion of economic performance should therefore be treated with caution. Moreover, measuring the relative efficiency of EC versus Japanese banks is still more problematic. Some analyses suggest that certain categories of Japanese banks did possess a number of important strengths *vis-à-vis* their EC competitors in the late 1980s, but other studies point out that they were also vulnerable in a number of important respects. See, for example, Gabriel Hawawini and Michael Schill, 'The Japanese Presence in the European Financial Services Sector,' but also the corresponding 'The Japanese Presence in the European Financial Services Sector: Comment' of Gunter Dufey in Mark Mason and Dennis Encarnation (eds.), *Does Ownership Matter? Japanese Multinationals in Europe* (Oxford: Oxford University Press, 1994), ch. 7.

8. Calculated from data as cited in Neven, 'Structural Adjustment in European Retail Banking,' 173.

9. Ibid.

10. Data as cited in Franco Bruni, 'Banking and Financial Reregulation towards 1992: The Italian Case,' in Dermine (ed.), *European Banking in the 1990s*, 239. Percentages rounded to the nearest whole number. For other measures of profitability, see, for example, Ramon Caminal, Jordi Gual, and Xavier Vives, 'Competition in Spanish Banking,' and Antonio M. Borges, 'Portuguese Banking in the Single European Market,' both in Dermine (ed.), *European Banking in the 1990s*, 284, 344.

11. For a typology of government controls in the banking industry, see Ingo Walter, *Barriers to Trade in Banking and Financial Services* (London: Trade

Policy Research Centre, 1985), ch. 1. On the distinctions between regulation and supervision, see Louis Pauly, 'Institutionalizing a Stalemate: National Financial Policies and the International Debt Crisis,' *Journal of Public Policy*, 10: 1 (1990). In addition to differing regulatory regimes, member states also differed with respect to their degrees of direct government involvement in the banking sector. In France, for example, two of the three largest French-based banks were controlled by the state, whereas in the United Kingdom the state held no such position.

12. The Danish government also apparently placed relatively few such controls on local banks. See Rob Dixon, *Banking in Europe: The Single Market* (London: Routledge, 1991), ch. 1.

13. On the development of the British banking industry and its relations with the state, see Forrest Caprie, 'The Evolving Regulatory Framework in British Banking,' in Martin Chick (ed.), *Governments, Industries and Markets* (London: Edward Elgar, 1990), ch. 7; Geoffrey Jones, 'Competition and Competitiveness in British Banking, 1918–71,' in Geoffrey Jones and Maurice Kirby (eds.), *Competitiveness and the State: Government and Business in Twentieth-Century Britain* (Manchester: Manchester University Press, 1991), ch. 7. On the historical development of British multinational banks see, in particular, Geoffrey Jones, *British Multinational Banking, 1830–1990* (Oxford: Oxford University Press, 1993).

14. See, for example, Colin Mayer, 'The Regulation of Financial Services: Lessons from the United Kingdom for 1992,' in Dermine (ed.), *European Banking in the 1990s*, ch. 2. For a survey of post-war British banking regulation, see J. S. Fforde, 'Competition, Innovation and Regulation in British Banking,' *Bank of England Quarterly*, 23: 3 (Sept. 1983), 363–76. On contemporary UK banking principles, see *Banking Act 1987: Section 16: Statement of Principles* (London: Bank of England, May 1988).

15. Dixon, *Banking in Europe*, ch. 1.

16. Treaty Establishing the European Economic Community, Mar. 25, 1957. On financial integration and related matters, see Treaty Articles 52, 59, 67–73. For an illuminating early attempt to predict the process of financial integration in the EC, see Hans O. Schmitt, 'Capital Markets and the Unification of Europe,' *World Politics*, 20: 2 (Jan. 1968), 228–44.

17. Ernst Baltensperger and Jean Dermine, 'European Banking: Prudential and Regulatory Issues,' in Dermine (ed.), *European Banking in the 1990s*, 20.

18. Council Directive 77/780/EEC: First Council Directive of Dec. 12, 1977 on the coordination of laws, regulations, and administrative provisions relating to the taking up and pursuit of the business of credit institutions. Under the home country control provision (and following the precedent created by the *Cassis de Dijon* case), the home country of the parent bank—rather than the host country of the foreign subsidiary—would assume primary supervisory powers.

19. See Paolo Clarotti, 'Progress and Future Development of Establishment and Services in the EC in Relation to Banking,' *Journal of Common Market Studies*, 22: 3 (Mar. 1984), 213.

20. Baltensperger and Dermine, 'European Banking,' 22.

21. L. Rita Theil, 'Banking in the Single Market: Strategic Decisions for Non-EC Banks,' *Butterworths Journal of International Banking and Financial Law*, 8: 1 (Jan. 1993), 27.

22. On the progressive international expansion of Japanese banks in the post-war era see, in particular, Japan, Ministry of Finance, *Ginkokyoku kinyu nenpo* (Annual financial report of the banking division) (Tokyo, annual).

23. Indeed, 'a fundamental facet of the Japanese political economy,' as one scholar has rightly observed, 'is that financial markets are considered too important to be left to the free play of market forces.' Dufey, 'Comment.'

24. For details of this process, see Goto Shinichi, *Toshi ginko* (Investment banks) (Tokyo: Kyoikusha, 1976), 177.

25. The following discussion is drawn largely from Takashi Kiuchi, 'Japanese Investment Strategies in the EC Banking Industry,' a paper presented at the conference 'Japanese Direct Investment in a Unifying Europe: Impacts on Japan and the European Community,' Fontainebleau, June 1992. See also the historical discussion in Hidenari Hirota, 'The Attitude of Japanese Banks towards a Single European Market in 1992,' *Revue de la Banque/Bank-en Financiewezen* (Jan. 1990), 17–20.

26. On additional (and evolving) motivations for Japanese bank expansion in European markets during the 1970s, see F. N. Burton and F. H. Saelens, 'The European Investments of Japanese Financial Institutions,' *Columbia Journal of World Business* (Winter 1986), 27–33.

27. On the evolution of Japanese banking deregulation from the early 1980s, see Federation of Bankers Associations of Japan, *Japanese Banks '92* (Tokyo: 1992), 10–14.

28. Indeed, in the 1980s the vast majority of Japanese banks' business dealings carried out through UK branches and subsidiaries involved international rather than UK-oriented transactions. See Henry Terrell, Robert Dohner, and Barbara Lowrey, 'The Activities of Japanese Banks in the United Kingdom and in the United States, 1980–1988,' *Federal Reserve Bulletin*, 76: 2 (Feb. 1990), 41–2; R. J. Walton and Dermot Trimble, 'Japanese Banks in London,' *Bank of England Quarterly*, 27: 4 (Nov. 1987), 519–20. On Japanese participation in Euromarkets in the City of London during the 1980s, see, in particular, Watanabe Shigeaki, *Za shitei kemmon roku* (Observations on the City) (Tokyo: Nihon keizai shinposha, 1990).

29. For a more detailed discussion of the motivations for Japanese banks to expand their operations in Europe during the 1980s, see Burton and Saelens, 'The European Investments of Japanese Financial Institutions,' 27–33; Dufey, 'Comment'; J. Thorstein Duser, *International Strategies of Japanese*

Banks: The European Perspective (London: Macmillan, 1990), ch. 3; Hawawini and Schill, 'The Japanese Presence in the European Financial Services Sector'; Hirota, 'The Attitude of Japanese Banks towards a Single European Market in 1992,' 17–20; Kiuchi, 'Japanese Investment Strategies in the EC Banking Industry.'

30. On the expansion of Japanese banks in London more generally, see Hamada Yasuyuki and Sawada Takashi, *Togin rondon shiten* (The London branches of Japanese banks) (Tokyo: Toyo keizai shinposha, 1992), ch. 3.

31. Official data as cited in Terrell, Dohner, and Lowrey, 'The Activities of Japanese Banks in the United Kingdom and in the United States, 1980–1988,' 40.

32. Duser, *International Strategies of Japanese Banks*, 110. Duser also noted a substantial increase in the number of Japanese representative offices in the EC during these years.

33. On the movement of Japanese banks into southern Europe see, for example, Anthony Crowley, 'A Southern Spree,' *Far Eastern Economic Review* (Aug. 3, 1989), 55.

34. On the dimensions of Japanese bank expansion in the EC during the 1980s see, in particular, Duser, *International Strategies of Japanese Banks*, ch. 3; Hawawini and Schill, 'The Japanese Presence in the European Financial Services Sector'; Terrell, Dohner, and Lowrey, 'The Activities of Japanese Banks in the United Kingdom and in the United States, 1980–1988,' 39–49; Walton and Trimble, 'Japanese Banks in London,' 519–24. Japanese banks also significantly expanded their European operations in (non-EC) Switzerland during this period.

35. For a contemporaneous overview of the development of foreign banks in Japan, see Brian W. Semkow, 'Foreign Financial Institutions in Japan: Legal and Financial Barriers and Opportunities: Part 1,' *Butterworths Journal of International Banking and Financial Law*, 8: 2 (Feb. 1993), 62–7.

36. Data as cited in R. M. Pecchioli, *The Internationalisation of Banking: The Policy Issues* (Paris: Organization for Economic Cooperation and Development, 1983), 69.

37. Commission of the European Communities, Directorate-General for Financial Institutions and Company Law, 'Treatment Accorded in Third Countries to Community Credit Institutions and Insurance Companies: Japan,' unpublished report (Brussels, June 26, 1992), 4–5.

38. 'French feutre,' *Banker* (Aug. 1987), 26.

39. Interview with Patricia Jackson, Bank of England, Mar. 1993; *Financial Times*, Feb. 16, 1990. On related British actions, see 'Japanese Win a Six-Year Fight,' *Euromoney* (Apr. 1987), 123.

40. As quoted in *Banker* (Apr. 1988). For more substantial Japanese perspectives on the EC integration process and its implications for Japanese firms, see '1992 nen EC ikinai shijo togo o meguru ugoki ni tsuite' (On the

movement towards 1992 EC internal market unification), in Bank of Japan, *Chosa geppo* (Monthly research report), 1 (Jan. 1989), 23–47; Aizawa Koetsu, *EC no kinyu togo* (EC financial integration) (Tokyo: Toyo keizai shinposha, 1990), especially chs. 1–3, 8.

41. Commission Notice No. 88/C 84/01: Proposal for a second council directive on the coordination of laws, regulations, and administrative provisions relating to the taking up and pursuit of the business of credit institutions and amending Directive 77/80/EEC. For a useful overview of EC financial integration, see Dominique Servais, *The Single Financial Market* (2nd edn., Luxembourg: Office for Official Publications of the European Communities, 1991).

42. Interviews with current and former members of DG XV directly involved in the drafting process, Brussels, Mar. 1993; *Financial Times*, June 7, 1988.

43. Branches were not covered in this draft legislation (nor in any subsequent versions) because Article 59 of the Treaty of Rome accords them neither the right of establishment nor the freedom to provide services.

44. Georgios Zavvos, 'EC Strategy for the Banking Sector: The Perspective of 1992,' *European Affairs* (Jan. 1988), 108; EC Office of Press and Public Affairs, 'EC Commission Clarifies Reciprocity Provisions in Proposed Second Banking Directive,' mimeo (Washington, Apr. 13, 1989).

45. In addition, the vague wording of the draft left open the possibility that the Commission could apply reciprocity universally rather than only in the specific sector in question. Thus, for example, a finding that the Japanese did not provide reciprocal access for EC banks in Japan could then empower the Commission to deny Japanese firms operating in a different sector, such as automobiles, reciprocal access to Community markets.

46. *Financial Times*, Apr. 14, 1989.

47. Interview with former official of DG XV.

48. Hirota, 'The Attitude of Japanese Banks towards a Single European Market in 1992,' 19.

49. Testimony of Ishihara Hideo before the Subcommittee on Financial Institutions, Supervision, Regulation, and Insurance of the US House of Representatives (Washington, Sept. 1989).

50. Okabe Yoji, as quoted in 'EC Law Shapes the Pattern of Banking,' *Euromoney* (June 1989), 64.

51. Indeed, these criticisms are consistent with a larger pattern of US opposition to strict reciprocity in the banking industry, for the durability of interstate and other American barriers suggests that achievement of true reciprocity for European banks in the US remains a distant goal at best. See Louis Pauly, *Opening Financial Markets: Banking Politics in the Pacific Rim* (Ithaca, NY: Cornell University Press, 1985), ch. 3.

52. Letter, Edward J. Streator, President, American Chamber of Commerce

(United Kingdom), to Phillippe Wacker, EC Affairs Office, American Chamber of Commerce in Belgium, Feb. 1, 1989.

53. *Financial Times*, Nov. 3, 1988. See, also, 'Proposed EC Second Banking Coordination Directive: U.S. Comments,' May 16, 1989, a démarche of the United States government sent to all EC member states and to the Commission.

54. Willy DeClerq (LDR), MEP, as quoted in European Parliament, *Session Documents* (Nov. 20, 1989), 16.

55. Matthew Crabbe, 'EC Law Shapes the Pattern of European Banking,' *Euromoney* (June 1989), 63.

56. See, also, *Financial Times*, June 7, 1988.

57. Letter, Jeremy Morse to Leon Brittan, Mar. 6, 1989. In his letter, Morse also expressed the Federation's concern over the lack of a clear definition of reciprocity in the proposed directive. See, in addition, the commentary in Banking Federation of the European Community, *Annual Report: 1988*, 10 and *Annual Report: 1989*, 28–9.

58. 'Formally, foreign banks in Japan enjoy national treatment in many fields,' the report stated. 'For a variety of reasons, however, they have only limited access to the Japanese market.' As quoted in *Financial Times*, Aug. 17, 1989. Although the Federation's report identified restrictions in twenty-five other non-EC countries in addition to those in Japan, the *Financial Times* noted, 'the most detailed complaints are levelled against Japan.'

59. *Financial Times*, Nov. 7, 1988. Among EC states, the Netherlands and Germany offered strong support for the views propounded by the UK and Luxembourg. Dixon, *Banking in Europe*, 66.

60. As quoted in *Financial Times*, Sept. 24–5, 1988.

61. Ibid. Indeed, it was reported that the UK and Luxembourg, which believed they held a major 'competitive edge' as hosts to the international financial services industry, had forged a 'tactical alliance' to fight the proposal for central administration of reciprocity measures. Neither country, it was reported, 'wants that edge blunted by over-regulation or [other] interference from Brussels.' *Financial Times*, Nov. 7, 1988.

62. George S. Zavvos, 'Banking Integration and 1992: Legal Issues and Policy Implications,' *Harvard International Law Journal*, 31: 2 (Spring 1990), 493.

63. Philippe Vigneron and Aubry Smith, 'The Concept of Reciprocity in Community Legislation: The Example of the Second Banking Directive,' *Journal of International Banking Law*, 5 (1990), 183. This action followed the Commission's Nov. 1988 statement that the proposed measures would not apply to previously established third-country subsidiaries in the Community, as well as the decision of Community Finance Ministers meeting in Council that same month to return the draft proposal to the Commission for modification.

64. European Parliament, *Session Documents*, various issues; *Financial Times*, June 21, 1989. The autumn 1989 debates in the European Parliament (EP) constituted a second reading, preceded the previous year by the EP's first such series of deliberations.

65. For detailed discussion of these modifications see, in particular, Paolo Clarotti, 'Un pas décisif vers le marché commun des banques: La Deuxième Directive de coordination en matière d'établissements de crédit' (A decisive step towards the Common Market for banks: the Second Coordination Directive concerning credit establishments), *Revue du marché commun*, 330 (Sept.–Oct. 1989), esp. 457–8; Vigneron and Smith, 'The Concept of Reciprocity in Community Legislation,' 181–91; Marc Dassesse, 'The Single Banking Market of 1993,' *EIU European Trends*, 4 (1989), 75–6. On the more general question of Community competence in the domain of international trade in services, see Philippe Vigneron and Aubry Smith, 'Le Fondement de la compétence communitaire en matière de commerce international de services' (The foundations of Community competence concerning trade in international services), *Cahiers de droit européen*, 5–6 (1992), 515–64.

66. Apparently to avoid usage of the politically sensitive term 'reciprocity,' however, the final version of 2BCD refers only to 'relations with third countries.' Vigneron and Smith, 'The Concept of Reciprocity in Community Legislation,' 183, 187.

67. See, for example, Loukas Tsoukalis, *The New European Community: The Politics and Economics of Integration* (2nd rev. edn., Oxford: Oxford University Press, 1993), 304–5.

68. In addition, the Community also apparently ruled out the possibility of universal reciprocity, affirming that such reciprocity rather would be imposed only in the same (financial services) sector. For further discussion of the meaning of reciprocity as contained in the 2BCD, see, in particular, Zavvos, 'Banking Integration and 1992,' esp. 493–7. On reciprocity and the 2BCD see also Douglas Croham, *Reciprocity and the Unification of the European Banking Market*, Group of Thirty Occasional Papers 27 (New York: Group of Thirty, 1989); Richard Dale, *International Banking Deregulation: The Great Banking Experiment* (Oxford: Blackwell, 1992), ch. 10; Sydney Key, 'Mutual Recognition: Integration of the Financial Sector in the European Community,' *Federal Reserve Bulletin*, 75: 9 (Sept. 1989), esp. 599–601, 608–9; David Llewllyn, 'Financial Services and Competition,' *Banking World* (Feb. 1989), 28–34; Hal S. Scott, 'Reciprocity and the Second Banking Directive,' in Ross Cranston (ed.), *Single Market and the Law of Banking* (London: Lloyd's of London Press, 1991), ch. 4.

69. The Council then decides such Commission requests by qualified majority voting.

70. A finding of third-country failure to provide neither de facto 'national treatment' nor 'effective market access' could be based either on the

Commission's own analyses as described above, or on 'other information.' See Pargraph 4, Article 9.

71. Ibid.

72. The Commission did spell out, in June 1992, more detailed definitions of 'national treatment' and 'effective market access.' See Commission of the European Communities, 'Treatment Accorded in Third Countries . . . Japan,' 6. Nonetheless, ambiguities remain. Indeed, 'national treatment is almost as vague a concept as reciprocity itself,' the *Financial Times* (Apr. 14, 1989) pointed out in assessing third-country measures in the 2BCD. 'How do you measure relative degrees of market access when the structure of European and Japanese financial markets is so different?'

73. Indeed, the entire Directive, stemming from the precedent of the 1BCD, is based on the principle of home country control. This principle, as previously noted, delegates to concerned member states the primary authority to supervise financial institutions operating within their borders.

74. Commission of the European Communities, 'Treatment Accorded in Third Countries . . . Japan,' 15, n. *.

75. See Commission of the European Communities, Directorate-General for Financial Institutions and Company Law, 'Treatment Accorded in Third Countries to Community Credit Institutions and Insurance Companies: Report by the Commission to the Council,' mimeo (Brussels, June 22, 1992), 1.

76. Dassesse, 'The Single Banking Market of 1993,' 75.

77. Sir Leon Brittan, 'Financial Services after 1992: Towards Global Leadership,' in EC Committee of the American Chamber of Commerce, *EC Financial Services Guide* (Brussels: American Chamber of Commerce in Belgium, 1992), 2. Further confusion initially arose because some member states were slow to implement provisions of the 2BCD in domestic legislation. See Karel Lanoo, 'Implementation of Financial Services Directives,' unpublished report (Center for European Policy Studies, Brussels, Mar. 25, 1993), 4 and Table 1.

78. Indeed, at least one observer believes that member states might well be able to exercise such informal means even in preventing the acquisition of a local bank by a credit institution based in another EC member state. See Tony Shea, 'European Banking in the 1990s,' *Butterworths Journal of International Banking and Financial Law*, 8: 1 (Jan. 1993), 9.

79. Committee on Financial Markets, Directorate for Financial, Fiscal and Enterprise Affairs, OECD, 'Liberalisation of Capital Markets and Access to the Community by Third Country Financial Institutions,' unpublished draft (Feb. 16, 1993), 5–6. For additional scenarios which might hinder third-country bank access to EC financial markets, see, for example, Theil, 'Banking in the Single Market,' 28–9.

80. The Commission did note, however, that the Japanese government was in

the process of dismantling many barriers which had maintained this separation.

81. Commission of the European Communities, 'Treatment Accorded in Third Countries . . . Japan,' 1–7.

82. On the evolution of the Japanese regulatory environment for foreign banks, see Pauly, *Opening Financial Markets*, ch. 4.

83. Ibid., 1. The Commission made similar recommendations regarding US financial markets.

84. On various problems at Japanese banks together with resulting European reactions see, for example, *Banker* (Jan. 1991), 50 and (Jan. 1992), 36; *Euromoney* (July 1992), Supplement, 7–12.

85. *Financial Times*, July 27, 1995; *Wall Street Journal*, July 27, 1995.

86. Interview with Paolo Clarotti, Chief of Division, Banks and Financial Institutions, DG XV, Brussels, Mar. 1993.

87. As quoted in *Daily Telegraph*, Feb. 18, 1992.

88. Ibid. See, also, the comments of Georgios Zavvos in Center for European Policy Studies, 'Proceedings of the Seminar on Financial Market Liberalisation after 1992: Problems and Priorities,' mimeo (Dec. 3, 1992), 1–2.

89. The Community had apparently adopted a similar approach in the securities and insurance sectors as well. See Commission of the European Communities, 'Treatment Accorded in Third Countries . . .' Report by the Commission,' 10–16.

90. *New York Times*, Oct. 1, 1989, *Wall Street Journal*, Oct. 12, 1989, and Mira Wilkins, 'Japanese Multinationals in the United States: Continuity and Change, 1879–1990,' *Business History Review*, 64 (Winter 1990).

91. Edward Graham and Paul Krugman, *Foreign Direct Investment in the United States* (2nd edn., Washington: Institute for International Economics, 1991), 30.

92. US Department of the Treasury, *National Treatment Study* (Washington, D.C.: Department of the Treasury, 1994), 16.

93. Ibid., 14–15.

94. On state banking restrictions and their effects on foreign banks in the United States, see William Jackson, 'Foreign Investment in American Banking: Competitiveness, Legislation and Regulation,' unpublished report (Congressional Research Service, Aug. 8, 1994).

5

The Regulation of Multinationals in Comparative Perspective

JAPAN directly invested enormous sums of capital in Europe beginning in the late 1980s. Historically the recipient of only limited inflows of such FDI, European officials debated appropriate policy responses to this suddenly explosive growth. The ultimate character of those responses was largely consistent across critically affected sectors examined in this study, yet differed greatly from analogous American policy responses. This record points to the operation of a more general European policy model towards the Japanese Challenge. Moreover, comparing this European record with analogous Japanese as well as American responses offers fresh insights into ongoing debates over the notion of convergence of capitalist systems across the entire Triad of advanced industrialized countries.

EUROPEAN RESPONSE

The fundamental nature of European policy towards direct investment from Japan had become clear by the time the Single Market had entered into effect. In the automobile sector, critical aspects of that policy were contained in the 'Elements of Consensus' and related understandings. Through the 'Elements,' the EC had managed effectively to limit imports of cars from Japan entering both the Community as a whole and five specified EC markets until the year 2000. And through related arrangements, moreover, the Community had placed implicit restrictions on the production and export behavior of Japanese auto transplant factories operating within the Community. In addition, individual EC member states such as Great Britain imposed their own, nominally 'voluntary,' controls on the behavior of Japanese auto transplants functioning within their territories. Here, then, was a clear demonstration of strongly interventionist European policies adopted to confront one critical instance of the wider Japanese Challenge.

A similar European approach emerges from the pattern of policymaking towards Japanese FDI and related trade in the region's consumer electronics industry. Following a model of public intervention first crafted to meet growing Japanese competition in the color television sector, individual European states or the Community as a whole placed major restrictions first on imports of Japanese consumer electronics products and later on the local operations of Japanese transplant factories. In the color TV sector, for example, the imposition of tariffs and quotas on Japanese imports was followed by local content and other performance requirements on Japanese firms manufacturing within these restricted European markets.

With regard to videocassette recorders, rising Japanese import penetration was met by individual member-state restrictions, such as Spanish trade quotas and French inspection procedures, followed by direct intervention from the European Commission to restrict quantities of Japanese VCR imports and set minimum prices for such imports and, still later, to boost tariffs on these goods. When Japanese firms then opted to establish VCR manufacturing facilities within Europe, the Commission effectively imposed local content controls through enactment of import restrictions on unassembled VCR kits and by threatening (and later imposing) antidumping penalties on Japanese VCR transplants which sourced less than 40 per cent of the value of their inputs from local suppliers. Community members such as France and Great Britain then added their own performance requirements on Japanese VCR plants producing within their borders. Much the same pattern emerged in the compact disc player sector as well.

Nor was the restrictive character of European policymaking towards the Japanese limited to the manufacturing sector. On the contrary, European authorities crafted broadly similar approaches to confront the perceived Japanese Challenge in the critically important banking sector as well. As Japan's banking presence continued to grow in London and elsewhere in the Community during the late 1980s, the Commission initiated a policy process which led to the eventual adoption of the Second Banking Coordination Directive. Although, in its final form, this Directive placed no immediate restrictions on Japanese banks in the Community, it did empower the EC to limit new entries of such institutions if Japan failed to meet certain specified standards of reciprocal access.[1] In addition, individual member states retained wide-ranging powers to regulate the entry and operation of Japanese banks within their national economies.

In sum, the European Community and its member states together adopted a broad range of restrictive policies designed to meet the Japanese Challenge to European markets. Although the precise nature of these measures differed by sector or product, in the critically important automobile, consumer electronics, and banking sectors European officials responded to the Japanese Challenge by threatening and often imposing major public restrictions on competition from Japan at the regional and national levels.

EUROPE, AMERICA, AND THE JAPANESE CHALLENGE

How does the European approach towards the Japanese Challenge compare to the analogous American approach? Here again, an examination of policy actions towards Japanese competition in three key sectors reveals strikingly consistent patterns.

Consider, for example, the automobile industry. In 1981 the United States negotiated its own bilateral auto accord with the Japanese, which set limits on the volume of imported Japanese cars and certain other categories of motor vehicles for three years. Yet unlike the Europeans, who obliged the Japanese to limit auto exports to their region until the year 2000, the Americans allowed their export restraint agreement with the Japanese to lapse, after a one-year extension, in 1985. And again unlike the Europeans in their policy arrangements with the Japanese, through its bilateral accord the United States in no way linked the operation of Japanese transplants in the United States with Japanese exports to the American market. Nor did the US government in general impose any other restraints on Japan's auto FDI in America in subsequent years. Indeed, rather than seeking to restrict Japanese automobile investments in the United States, as suggested above individual American states actively *encouraged* Japanese FDI through the provision of tax breaks and other incentives.[2] Japanese automakers, in short, confronted a very different policy environment as they sought to expand their presence in the economies of each of their two Triad partners.

American and European policy approaches similarly contrast in the case of consumer electronics. Despite the continuing vulnerabilities of a declining US consumer electronics industry, the American government permitted unimpeded inflows of Japanese FDI into this sector. Moreover, individual states often provided attractive incentive packages to Japanese investors yet in general did not link them to performance requirements. And again in contrast to their European counterparts, US officials offered no direct subsidies to the dwindling number of local firms in the industry as they confronted growing Japanese FDI. Partly as a result, through acquisitions and greenfield projects Japanese FDI poured into the American consumer electronics industry in unprecedented quantities, and subsequently operated without the conditions attached to similar Japanese direct investments in the European Community. And with respect to Japanese import competition, the US government intervened only in a few specific cases where domestic producers could demonstrate clear instances of Japanese dumping.

Although the contrast is less stark in the banking sector, here again the Europeans adopted stronger policy measures in response to the local build-up of Japanese firms. Through legislative and other means the US government and individual American states have, of course, long regulated the operation of the banking sector in ways which naturally affected the activities of foreign banks. Yet in contrast to the policies of many European countries, American states regarded as major financial centers maintained relatively open policies which enabled Japanese banks to expand aggressively. Moreover, although the US Congress hotly debated the proposal, ultimately the US government did not adopt European-style reciprocity standards which could be invoked against Japanese banks seeking entry into local markets.

In sum, European officials generally instituted more restrictive policies than did their American counterparts when each group confronted its own Japanese Challenge in these three critical industries. Although there are important instances of national or state intervention in America against Japanese competition in automobiles, consumer electronics, and banks during these years, such interventions in general proved far more limited than in the European case and rarely aimed to control Japan's direct investments. By contrast, in each of these sectors European policymakers explicitly threatened and often imposed major controls over Japanese direct investments as well as exports to their region.

This overall pattern of European policymaking points to the operation of a more general policy model towards the Japanese Challenge. This model is defined in part by a set of contextual features present in the European environment, some of which also existed in the United States.

One feature broadly common to Europe and the United States was the particular historical development of Japanese FDI in both regions. Beginning in the late 1800s and lasting for almost a century thereafter, Japanese firms directly invested only minor amounts of capital in these two Western markets. In addition to their paucity, in Europe and the United States these investments were heavily concentrated in the services sector, usually entered only a few specific locales, were generally undertaken to facilitate flows of trade and technology, and shared other common attributes as well.

Yet in both Europe and the United States, in the relatively recent past many critical characteristics of Japanese FDI changed dramatically as compared with this century-old pattern. In recent years amounts of FDI from Japan vastly increased to both regions, for example, their sectoral composition shifted towards greater proportions in non-service sectors, the internal locations of such investments became more diffuse, and the overseas production of goods and services to defend or enhance markets abroad, rather than the mere facilitation of trade and technology flows between these markets and Japan, became a more important motivation to undertake such investments. These changes in the nature of Japanese FDI in both regions raised considerable concern and stimulated lively policy debate on both sides of the Atlantic.

A second feature common to both Europe and the United States was a range of business and economic disadvantages of domestically owned firms, real or perceived, *vis-à-vis* Japanese competitors. In the automobile industry, for example, American and European business managers and government officials rightly believed that the operations of many of their domestic auto firms were significantly less competitive than those of Toyota, Nissan, Honda, and other counterparts from Japan. Much the same situation obtained in the consumer electronics sector, where local companies such as RCA and Zenith in the United States and Philips and Thomson in Europe faced major competitive threats from the likes of Japanese producers Sony and Matsushita. And although their fears greatly exaggerated the actual nature of the threat, American and European government officials and business managers warned that Japanese competitors posed major threats to the health of domestically-owned banks.

In addition to such shared attributes, there were in Europe at least two contextual features not present in the US environment which apparently help explain the distinctive nature of the European response. One key distinguishing feature was a Europe which was, at least in one important sense, a second mover. Although Japanese multinationals concentrated their European investments in many of the same industries in which they concentrated their American investments, in the automobile and certain other key industries Japanese FDI (and trade) initially surged into the United States rather than Europe.

As Japanese FDI in the United States steadily mounted, Europeans began to develop their own interpretations of the potential impact of such investment back in Europe. In particular, European officials tried to evaluate the effects of America's relatively open policies towards FDI and other forms of economic competition from Japan. Although there was a range of European reaction, many leading officials concluded that American policy interventions were inadequate, and that adoption of a similar approach in Europe would seriously harm local business and economic interests.

In automobiles, for example, European officials noted the coincidence of large-scale Japanese FDI in the United States with major increases in Japanese automobile market share in America and growing problems for America's Big Three. In consumer electronics, European authorities watched as rising Japanese FDI in the US reinforced Japan's already powerful position in that American industry and posed major new competitive threats to the dwindling number of US producers which continued to operate. And in banking, Community policymakers viewed with growing concern the rapid expansion of Japanese banks in California and elsewhere in the United States.

Based on their observations of American experiences in these and other sectors, European officials became increasingly concerned about the ultimate consequences for Europe of unregulated Japanese FDI and related trade in their own region. In short, prevailing Community interpretations of America's experience with Japanese economic competition contributed significantly to the shaping of EC policies towards Japan as Japanese FDI surged and the Community moved toward greater unification.

A second distinctive element in the European context was defined by a tradition of generally strong European states together with an increasingly powerful European Community able and often willing to intervene actively in the market to achieve desired policy outcomes.[3] The record of European state regulation of inward FDI, for example, is well known. When American multinationals poured large amounts of capital into Europe during the 1950s and 1960s, for instance, numerous European governments intervened often and vigorously to block, delay, or otherwise impede the free inflow or development of such FDI into local manufacturing and service sectors.[4]

Here again the automobile sector provides an important case in point. Successive post-war German governments, for example, provided subsidies and other support for Volkswagen and other domestically-owned auto firms as they confronted growing direct competition from the local subsidiaries of Ford and General Motors.[5] The French government not only provided direct and sustained support for Renault following its nationalization of that company in 1948, but also promoted the subsequent Citroën–Peugeot and Renault–Berliet mergers in efforts to shore up weaknesses among private-sector firms in the local industry as competition from America (and elsewhere) intensified. Moreover, the French specifically prevented both Ford and GM from establishing local subsidiaries in 1964.[6] And even post-war British governments encouraged defensive mergers and other actions to strengthen domestically-owned auto firms against growing competition from American multinationals. Nor is this European policy record toward the American Challenge confined to the automobile industry—or even exclusively to inward direct investment.[7]

By contrast, US policy towards inward FDI historically has been far less restrictive. Indeed, as far back as the late nineteenth and early twentieth centuries the US federal government generally confined FDI restrictions to 'especially sensitive sectors' such as communications, finance, and national defense. Although there was a variety of state laws which controlled inward FDI during these years, according to at least one noted scholar 'no attempt was ever made by state or federal authorities to monitor, much less control, all incoming or existing foreign investment.'[8]

Moreover, though limited controls persisted throughout the post-war period, in recent decades successive US administrations have issued explicit policy statements and taken other actions as well to support non-discriminatory treatment of FDI in the United States. This policy was articulated at least as early as 1977 by the Carter Administration, by the Reagan Administration in its 'International Investment Policy Statement' in 1983, by the Bush Administration in its 'United States Foreign Direct Investment Policy' in 1991, and by the Clinton Administration in a presidential speech in 1993.[9]

As they contemplated their response to Japan, European policymakers therefore drew upon distinctive historical traditions of relatively active public intervention to regulate FDI (and other forms of foreign economic competition) in domestic markets. Drawing in part on these traditions, Europe fashioned a set of policies towards the Japanese which largely resembled its policies designed to confront the rise of US multinationals during the American Challenge, but which greatly contrasted with the US policy response towards America's own Japanese Challenge.

Although EC member states clearly remained critical in Community policymaking towards Japan as unification approached, the role of the Commission became increasingly significant. The European political system had changed considerably since the days of the American Challenge. Though formally constituted through the Treaty of Rome, for many years the European Community remained a loose confederation of a relatively small number of independent states with limited spheres of coordination. Although the number of member states as well as their areas of policy coordination gradually expanded in subsequent years, from the mid-1980s the powers and responsibilities of the Commission and other Community institutions developed more quickly than in the past. Far more ambitious plans for European integration as contained in the 1992 program in particular vastly expanded the range of Community policy issues and the scope of Community authority.

The increasingly significant role of the EC greatly influenced European policymaking as the Japanese Challenge gathered force.

Although Community powers remained circumscribed and those of member states guaranteed through formal conventions and informal agreements, by the late 1980s the European Commission in particular began to emerge as a key regional actor in the creation of European policy towards Japan.

In automobiles, for example, the Commission not only initiated the broader European debate over policy towards Japanese automobile investment and trade in the region, but also critically influenced the ensuing policy process through both its intermediary position between member states and the Japanese government and its ability to sway member state positions with financial and regulatory carrots and sticks. Much the same pattern held for aspects of EC policymaking towards the rising Japanese consumer electronics presence in Europe, where the Commission initiated—and then significantly shaped—wider regional policymaking processes towards Japanese CTV, VCR, and CD player investment and trade in the Community.

And in banking as well, the Commission proved central to EC policymaking. The perception of a gathering Japanese banking challenge motivated key Commission officials initially to draft tough controls on Japanese banks in the region. Although these controls in their final form were significantly weakened, the Commission nonetheless remained central to the evolving policy process. Increasing European unification, in short, had significantly modified the policy environment in which Europe deliberated its policy options towards this new, Japanese challenge, and regional policy interests and proposed policy remedies were added to those at the national level.

This EC model was characterized not only by the active participation of the Commission in forging European policies towards the Japanese, but also by its direct role in carrying out policy decisions. At the time of the American Challenge, individual European states not only crafted their own policies towards the Americans, but also controlled their later implementation. By contrast, towards Japan the Commission played a critical role in monitoring, evaluating, and administering a whole host of European policies in the automobile, consumer electronics, and banking sectors.

In addition to these contextual elements, this model specifies a set of European policy actions at the regional and national levels. As Japanese investments mounted, European officials often instituted policies aimed at directly supporting locally established firms in their contests with Japanese competitors. These policies included direct state aid to local firms, government-backed research consortia, and other measures.

More important, however, was European imposition of major public controls over the entry and operation of Japanese multinationals in the region. When confronted with rising Japanese imports, European policymakers erected a whole series of trade impediments. And when confronted with surging Japanese FDI, European officials at the Community and national levels restricted or threatened to restrict Japanese firms in multifarious ways. These restrictions included explicit local content requirements and export performance standards and implicit limits on output volumes together with, in the banking sector, the potential imposition of public controls to prevent even the entry of Japanese firms into European markets in the absence of satisfactory reciprocal access.

In short, as Japanese investments mounted and unification approached, the Europeans crafted policies towards Japan which greatly contrasted with those adopted by the Americans. Based on a distinctive set of contextual features, in relative terms Europe chose restrictive regulation over open competition.

THE REGULATION OF MULTINATIONALS IN COMPARATIVE PERSPECTIVE

Yet the Europeans and the Americans have not been alone in confronting major foreign direct investment 'challenges' from abroad. Within the Triad, Japan also has confronted the specter of huge FDI inflows from powerful overseas competitors in recent times. Although many Western firms chose to concentrate their efforts and resources elsewhere, as early as the 1960s a significant and growing number of American and European MNCs attempted to invest directly in the Japanese market.[10] These firms operated in a variety of different industrial sectors, and included some of the largest, most internationally competitive companies in their respective fields of activity.[11]

In response to the potential inroads of such major Western multinationals, the Japanese government crafted policies designed to deter or prevent their entry through FDI. The centerpiece of this

Japanese policy was the Foreign Investment Law (FIL), which required prior approval for virtually all potential direct investments from abroad.[12] As administered throughout much of the postwar era, the FIL was used by Japanese officials to *dis*courage inflows of foreign direct investment but *en*courage inflows of foreign technology.[13] Each individual investment application under the FIL was rigorously scrutinized by numerous official agencies over long periods of time. Few applications ultimately were approved, attached to those few which did receive approval were onerous restrictions on the applicant firms' domestic activities, and many other potential investors simply were deterred even from applying for the requisite permissions.

Largely as a result of these policies, few American or European MNCs managed to directly invest in Japan during the post-war period. It is true that, among American firms, certain individual companies which possessed unique technologies, peculiar marketing skills, or other firm-specific assets managed to force their way into the Japanese market. Prominent examples of such firms include Coca-Cola, IBM, and Texas Instruments. Yet many other American MNCs which did not possess major ownership advantages or other powerful sources of leverage were simply locked out of the Japanese market as direct investors.[14]

Such local restrictions sharply curtailed the amount of FDI from the United States and Europe (and elsewhere) which penetrated the Japanese market during these years. Indeed, flows of FDI to Japan from the United States—the largest direct investor in Japan and throughout much of the rest of the world during the 1960s and early 1970s—rarely exceeded (and often fell far below) even $100 million in any single year during this period.[15] In fact, due substantially to Japanese restrictions on the entry of US firms, as late as 1975 Japan accounted for less than 3 per cent of the total stock of US FDI worldwide despite the growing size and importance of this key East Asian economy.[16]

Although Japanese policies towards inward FDI have become less restrictive in more recent years, the combination of certain persistent policy impediments together with the operation of other factors in the Japanese political economy continue substantially to limit foreign penetration of Japanese markets through direct investment. Despite the abolition of the FIL in 1980, for example, numerous Japanese laws continue explicitly to restrict FDI in key industries such as banking and securities, insurance, and telecommunications. In addition, through reservations entered under the OECD's Code of Liberalization of Capital Movements, Japanese authorities also continue sharply to curtail direct foreign participation in agriculture, forestry and fisheries, mining, petroleum, and other sensitive sectors. And finally, through other regulations and various informal practices Japanese policies further deter or impede FDI from abroad. Such regulations and practices include limited protection for intellectual property, lack of transparency, administrative guidance, and restricted access for foreign companies to bid on public procurement contracts.[17]

Even more significant in recent years, however, has been the operation of powerful, government-sanctioned restrictions on inward FDI which originates in the private sector.[18] Perhaps most significant have been impediments on foreign companies to merge with or acquire domestically-owned firms. High levels of cross-shareholdings between member firms of *keiretsu* business groups, unusual systems of corporate governance, small numbers of publicly traded shares of many important listed Japanese companies, and limited disclosure requirements for such firms have all effectively protected many important Japanese enterprises from the threat of foreign participation or outright foreign control. Added to these restrictive features of the Japanese political economy to direct investments from abroad are limits on access by foreign companies to influential private industry associations, the operation of complex distribution systems, and other factors.[19] Largely as a result of such impediments, as in the past Japan has continued to receive unusually small amounts of FDI in contrast to other advanced industrialized economies.[20]

This broader, comparative international perspective casts Europe in a somewhat different light. In response to surging Japanese investment inflows, as we have seen, American officials placed few restrictions on either the entry or operation of Japan-based MNCs, whereas authorities in Europe intervened often and actively, in general to regulate the local activities of Japanese firms. In response to even the potential for significant American and European investment inflows, on the other hand, Japan—first through explicit government policy and later through a combination of public and private means—impeded or deterred even the entry of many foreign MNCS into its local economy. Viewed in this wider perspective, the Europeans therefore proved more inclined to restrict inward FDI than the Americans but far less so than the Japanese.

These differing responses to inward direct investment in turn carry important implications for ongoing debates over the notion of convergence of the capitalist economies of the Triad. In recent years, as noted above, advocates of the convergence hypothesis have claimed that globalization, growing economic interdependence, and related factors have progressively eroded distinctive features of capitalism as practiced in the advanced industrialized economies. Such international factors, they argue, have instead forced these capitalist systems to behave in increasingly similar ways.

The case of inward direct investment examined in this study, however, offers little support for the convergence hypothesis. In contrast to the general predictions of the convergence school, America, Europe, and Japan continue to treat this critical aspect of foreign economic competition in clearly distinctive ways. As in earlier post-war decades, for example, the United States has maintained a relatively open regime towards inward FDI, whereas Japan continues to deter or impede even the entry of large amounts of direct investment from abroad. And Europe, again in contrast to the predictions of the convergence school, today remains neither as open as America nor as closed as Japan. Instead, Europe—like America and Japan—remains faithful to its own past.

NOTES

1. As noted in Ch. 4, however, in the mid-1990s the EC temporarily suspended the reciprocity clause of the 2BCD in the context of a multilateral financial services accord.

2. British and other European officials also provided incentives to Japanese auto transplants which invested in their locales, as noted in Ch. 2, yet they also imposed local content or other performance requirements on these investments.

3. Much of the literature on comparative political economy groups Great Britain with liberal America rather than other European nations in terms of state–market relations. See, for example, Peter Katzenstein, 'Domestic Structures and Strategies of Foreign Economic Policy,' in Peter Katzenstein (ed.), *Between Power and Plenty: Foreign Economic Policies of Advanced Indus-*

trialized States (Madison: University of Wisconsin Press, 1978) and John Zysman, *Governments, Markets and Growth: Financial Systems and the Politics of Industrial Change* (Ithaca, NY: Cornell University Press, 1983). At least with respect to their actions towards Japanese competition in the automobile and consumer electronics sectors examined in this study, however, levels of British government involvement in the economy more closely approximated Continental European rather than American state–market relations.

4. The following discussion of European policies designed to confront the post-war American Challenge is drawn from: Daniel Jones, *Maturity and Crisis in the European Car Industry: Structural Change and Public Policy* (Brighton: Sussex European Research Centre, 1981); Simon Reich, 'Roads to Follow: Regulating Foreign Direct Investment,' *International Organization*, 43:4 (Autumn 1989), 543–84 and id. *The Fruits of Fascism: Post-war Prosperity in Historical Perspective* (Ithaca, NY: Cornell University Press, 1990); Raymond Vernon, *Sovereignty at Bay: The Multinational Spread of U.S. Enterprises* (New York: Basic Books, 1971) and id., *Big Business and the State: Changing Relations in Western Europe* (Cambridge, Mass.: Harvard University Press, 1974).

5. According to Reich, during the 1960s and 1970s the German government also thwarted GM's attempts to purchase Daimler-Benz. See Reich, 'Roads to Follow,' 550–1.

6. However, the French authorities ultimately did not block Chrysler's acquisition of Simca the previous year.

7. Examples of European controls on US FDI in other sectors during the years of the American Challenge abound. When Mobil Oil sought to acquire the German firm Aral in 1967, for example, the German government limited the American company's control to 28% and demanded that Aral pass a resolution stating that 'the German identity of the firm shall be maintained.' Jean-Jacques Servan-Schreiber, *The American Challenge* (New York: Atheneum, 1968), 20. And, more generally, from the late 1950s until 1980 the French government apparently required prospective foreign investors in *every* sector to receive official permission from its Ministry of Finance before acquiring more than 20% of the shares in any French company. The Ministry further wielded the power to prevent foreign acquisitions of French firms if such acquisitions were deemed 'harmful to French interests or contrary to the government's industrial policy.' As quoted in Reich, 'Roads to Follow,' 555. European trade controls on US imports during the American Challenge were still more widespread. In addition to Community-wide tariffs, individual European governments impeded inflows of American goods and services in multifarious ways. See, for example, *New York Times*, May 25, 1968.

8. Mira Wilkins, *The History of Foreign Investment in the United States to 1914* (Cambridge, Mass.: Harvard University Press, 1989), 585.

9. On the exceptions to this general policy at the state as well as federal levels, see Edward Graham and Paul Krugman, *Foreign Direct Investment in the United States* (Washington: Institute for International Economics, 3rd edition, 1995), 122–3, 140–4.
10. Unless otherwise noted, the following account of FDI in Japan is based on Mark Mason, *American Multinationals and Japan: The Political Economy of Japanese Capital Controls, 1899–1980* (Cambridge, Mass.: Harvard University Press, 1992).
11. American multinationals in this group included such major firms as Coca-Cola, Dow Chemical, First National Bank, Ford, General Motors, IBM, Singer Sewing Machine, and Texas Instruments.
12. In the late 1950s the Japanese authorities created a limited exception which allowed certain foreign companies to invest directly in Japan without obtaining FIL approval. However, this alternative investment route did not provide for profit repatriation or other critical guarantees, and was in any case closed in 1964.
13. In practice, powerful Japanese business interests—generally seeking protection from major foreign competitors—often played a pivotal role in the administration of the FIL.
14. Well-known examples include Singer Sewing Machine, Fairchild, and various entry attempts by leading American chemical manufacturers.
15. Data from US Department of Commerce, *Selected Data on US Investment Abroad, 1950–76* (Washington: GPO, 1982).
16. Data from ibid., calculated on an historical cost basis.
17. Mark Mason, 'Japan's Low Levels of Inward Direct Investment: Causes, Consequences and Remedies,' in Edward K. Y. Chen and Peter Drysdale (eds.), *Corporate Links and Foreign Direct Investment in Asia and the Pacific* (Pymble: Harper Collins, 1995), 138–40.
18. Ibid., 140–2.
19. In addition, of course, several other important non-policy factors also have operated recently to limit FDI in Japan. These include the high costs of entering and operating in Japan—particularly after the spectacular post-Plaza rise in the value of the yen—and the emergence of significant investment opportunities in China and elsewhere in Asia.
20. As host to shares of total US FDI stocks throughout the world, for example, Japan still ranks far below numerous other major industrialized economies—despite the enormous size of the Japanese economy as compared to these other economies. Moreover, the global stock of FDI in Japan as a percentage of its GDP remains well below similar percentages in other major industrialized nations such as the United States, the United Kingdom, and Germany. Mason, 'Japan's Low Levels of Inward Direct Investment,' 130–3.

APPENDIX I

Local Content Arrangements in the United Kingdom

1. The United Kingdom has a long standing practice of establishing local content agreements with major inward investors in the vehicles sector. These are voluntary understandings between the company and the Government which establish targets for the level of local content in the particular model(s) being produced. These serve as an expression of commitment to a programme of investment which is of genuine and long term benefit to the UK and the European Community. They are also used as a tool for monitoring the development and impact of the project.

2. Inward investors voluntarily undertake to achieve local content levels of 60% at the start of commercial production rising to 80% within a specified period of time, normally two years. "Local" content represents EC (not UK) content and is calculated on the basis of a standard formula:

the ex-works price of the vehicle minus the value of components and materials originating outside the EC

divided by

the ex-works price of the vehicle.

3. The detailed definitions of the various elements involved in the calculation is set out in the Annex attached. [See note below.]

4. The figures for local content provided regularly by companies to the DTI [Department of Trade and Industry] are all subject to verification by an independent auditor. The companies concerned have all voluntarily agreed to abide by a set of standards established by DTI to ensure that the system and procedures for monitoring local content operate effectively and can be verified by the auditor.

5. The calculation of local content has no direct role in determining the "origin" of products for trade purposes. The legal basis for determining origin in the European Community is the Community's non-preferential origin rules. These are set out in Council Regulation 802/68 and specify that the origin is "the country in which the last substantial process or operation that is economically justified was performed."'

Note: The Annex, not included here, provides precise guidelines for measurement of local content.

Source: Unpublished document made available to the author by the UK Department of Trade and Industry.

APPENDIX II

The Second Banking Coordination Directive, Title III: Relations with Third Countries

Article 8

The competent authorities of the Member States shall inform the Commission:

(a) of any authorization of a direct or indirect subsidiary one or more undertakings of which are governed by the laws of a third country. The Commission shall inform the Banking Advisory Committee accordingly;

(b) whenever such a parent undertaking acquires a holding in a Community credit institution such that the latter would become its subsidiary. The Commission shall inform the Banking Advisory Committee accordingly.

When authorization is granted to the direct or indirect subsidiary of one or more parent undertakings governed by the law of third countries, the structure of the group shall be specified in the notification which the competent authorities shall address to the Commission in accordance with Article 3 (7) of Directive 77/780/EEC.*

Article 9

1. The Member States shall inform the Commission of any general difficulties encountered by their credit institutions in establishing themselves or carrying on banking activities in a third country.

2. Initially no later than six months before the publication of this Directive and thereafter periodically, the Commission shall draw up a report examining the treatment accorded to Community credit institutions in third countries, in the terms referred to in paragraphs 3 and 4, as regards establishment and the carrying-on of banking activities, and the acquisition of holdings in third-country credit institutions. The Commission shall submit those reports to the Council, together with any appropriate proposals.

3. Whenever it appears to the Commission, either on the basis of the reports referred to in paragraph 2 or on the basis of other information, that a third

* First Council Directive of 12 December 1977 on the coordination of laws, regulations and administrative provisions relating to the taking up and pursuit of the business of credit institutions.

country is not granting Community credit institutions *effective market access* comparable to that granted by the Community to credit institutions from that third country, the Commission may submit proposals to the Council for the appropriate mandate for negotiation with a view to obtaining comparable competitive opportunities for Community credit institutions. The Council shall decide by a qualified majority.

4. Whenever it appears to the Commission, either on the basis of the reports referred to in paragraph 2 or on the basis of other information that Community credit institutions in a third country do not receive *national treatment* offering the same competitive opportunities as are available to domestic credit institutions and the conditions of effective market access are not fulfilled, the Commission may initiate negotiations to remedy the situation.

In the circumstances described in the first subparagraph, it may also be decided at any time, and in addition to initiating negotiations, in accordance with the procedure laid down in Article 22 (2)**, that the competent authorities of the Member States must limit or suspend their decisions regarding requests pending at the moment of the decision or future requests for authorizations and the acquisition of holdings by direct or indirect parent undertakings governed by the laws of the third country in question. The duration of the measures referred to may not exceed three months.

Before the end of that three-month period, and in the light of the results of the negotiations, the Council may, acting on a proposal from the Commission, decide by a qualified majority whether the measures shall be continued.

Such limitations or suspension may not apply to the setting up of subsidiaries by credit institutions or their subsidiaries duly authorized in the Community, or to the acquisition of holdings in Community credit institutions by such institutions or subsidiaries.

5. Whenever it appears to the Commission that one of the situations in paragraphs 3 or 4 obtain, the Member States shall inform it at its request:

(a) of any request for the authorization of a direct or indirect subsidiary one or more parent undertakings of which are governed by the laws of the third country in question;

(b) whenever they are informed in accordance with Article 11 that such an undertaking proposes to acquire a holding in a Community credit institution such that the latter would become its subsidiary.

** Article 22 (2) stipulates that a committee composed of representatives of Member States (and chaired by a non-voting representative of the Commission) shall assist the Commission in deciding whether or not to adopt certain proposed measures. If this committee agrees with such proposals, the Commission shall adopt them. If this committee disagrees with the proposals, the matter is then referred to the Council for final determination.

This obligation to provide information shall lapse whenever an agreement is reached with the third country referred to in paragraph 3 or 4 or when the measures referred to in the second and third subparagraphs of paragraph 4 cease to apply.

6. Measures taken pursuant to this Article shall comply with the Community's obligations under any international agreements, bilateral or multilateral, governing the taking-up and pursuit of the business of credit institutions.'

Note: Emphasis added.

Source: *Official Journal of the European Communities*, Dec. 30, 1989.

Index